The Art of Spiritual Warfare

Dick Bernal

The Art of
Spiritual Warfare

Copyright © 2017 by Dick Bernal

ISBN# 13: 978-0692945704

Printed in the United States of America

Published by
Jubilee Christian Center
175 Nortech Parkway
San Jose, California 95134
www.jubilee.org

DEDICATION

*Without my number one prayer warrior —
my wife, Carla, and her mother, Roberta, this
book would not have been written. I dedicate
this book in deep appreciation of them and
their support in my life for more than forty
years, as well as the support of my family: my
three wonderful children, Adam, Sarah, and
Jesse, and at last count, my four grandkids,
Nick, Hannah, Mike & Jaden.*

Joshua 5:13 – 6:2

And it came to pass, when Joshua was by Jericho, that he lifted his eyes and looked, and behold, a Man stood opposite him with His sword drawn in His hand. And Joshua went to Him and said to Him, "Are You for us or for our adversaries?" So He said, "No, but as Commander of the army of the Lord I have now come." And Joshua fell on his face to the earth and worshiped, and said to Him, "What does my Lord say to His servant?" Then the Commander of the Lord's army said to Joshua, "Take your sandal off your foot, for the place where you stand is holy." And Joshua did so.

Now Jericho was securely shut up because of the children of Israel; none went out, and none came in. And the Lord said to Joshua: "See! I have given Jericho into your hand, its king, and the mighty men of valor.

Revelation 19:11-16

Now I saw heaven opened, and behold, a white horse. And He who sat on him was called Faithful and True, and in righteousness He judges and makes war. His eyes were like a flame of fire, and on His head were many crowns. He had a name written that no one knew except Himself. He was clothed with a robe dipped in blood, and His name is called The Word of God. And the armies in heaven, clothed in fine linen, white and clean, followed Him on white horses. Now out of His mouth goes a sharp sword, that with it He should strike the nations. And He Himself will rule them with a rod of iron. He Himself treads the winepress of the fierceness and wrath of Almighty God. And He has on His robe and on His thigh a name written:

KING OF KINGS AND
LORD OF LORDS.

CONTENTS

"In these last days,
God is moving
mightily by His
Spirit, and is
commanding us
to arise, to cross
over, to engage
in battle, and to
possess the land."

— *David Yonggi Cho*

FOREWARD

By Dr. David Yonggi Cho
Yoida Full Gospel Church
Seoul, Korea

We are living upon the threshold of a historical landmark in the Church Age. For this reason, I have always considered myself extremely fortunate to be able to serve God in these critical times. In these last days, God is moving mightily by His Spirit, and is commanding us to *arise, to cross over, to engage in battle, and to possess the land.* God is raising up a great army to accomplish His purposes in our generation.

Dick Bernal is a hungry tiger, whom God has raised up to purge the skies and pull down strongholds. He walks on the frontlines and on the cutting edge of this awesome move of God to destroy the works of the enemy. His first book, *Storming Hell's Brazen Gates,* was birthed when he and Dr. Paul Kim (my "Timothy" and former prominent lawyer turned venture capitalist, whom I sent to help build Pastor Bernal's Jubilee Christian Center in San Jose, California), were flying into Korea for our annual Church Growth International Conference. Dick experienced a great inspiration from the Lord regarding city-taking and the pulling down of strongholds. I believe the principles that Dick Bernal has outlined in this new book can revolutionize

13

and empower the church of America to rise up and take the land!

My ministry started with city-taking. When I first pioneered my church, nobody would come to our old, torn marine tent because there was great demonic oppression over the village. The key to breaking that bondage was the casting out of a demon from a woman who had lain paralyzed for seven years. When, after months of prayer, the demon oppressing her was cast out and she was healed, our church exploded with growth.

The sky above the village was broken open and the blessings of God began pouring down.

The growth of our church and the growth of Christianity throughout the nation of Korea did not come by accident. It came through fervent, violent, prevailing prayer. As Jesus said in Matthew 11:12, *"The Kingdom of Heaven suffers violence, and the violent take it by force."* For example, in our church we have all night prayer meetings every single evening where thousands come to pray. On Friday evenings, more than fifteen thousand people join hearts and hands to pray for the Kingdom of God to come. On Prayer Mountain, at least three thousand people are praying, fasting, and ministering unto the Lord on any given day. In all, one-and-a-half million people visit and pray there in any given year. This is not limited only to our church; all over South Korea, Christians are praying. One of the most unique characteristics of the Korean church is that millions gather early every morning at 5:30 a.m. to pray, despite wind, rain or snow.

Great sacrifices were made by the Korean church. The Kingdom of God indeed suffered violence. There was a long history of persecuting Christians by the Communists, as well as by the Japanese occupation forces. For instance, the Japanese installed Shinto altars in all Christian churches. The military police stood guard to enforce the law that required all Christians to bow down to the Shinto altar before entering to worship Almighty God. Those who refused were jailed and punished severely, with many ministers being executed at the hands of the Japanese forces. Many churches corporately decided to oppose this injustice. Many such churches were locked, with women and children inside, and burned to the ground due to their refusal to worship idols. Until recently, it took great sacrifice to be a Christian in Korea. Believers were a minority. But now, because the blood of the martyrs is the seed of the church, we count at least one-fourth of our nation to be believers in the Lord Jesus Christ.

Finally, a word of admonition. It is so necessary for those who are called to engage in this spiritual warfare to be holy and sanctified, because He is a holy God. Many who have cast out demons, who have prophesied, and who have done wonders in His name may find God declaring, "Depart from me you who practice lawlessness, I never knew you." The devil has crept into the Church and promoted iniquity, lawlessness and unrighteousness in our midst.

" Finally, my brethren, be strong in the Lord and in the power of His might. Put on the whole armor of God, that you may be able to stand against the wiles of the devil."

— *Ephesians 6:10*

It breaks my heart to see so many co-workers from the Kingdom falling in disgrace. Like the seven sons of Sceva, the evil spirit leapt upon them, overpowered them, prevailed against them, and they fled out of their homes naked and wounded. Without holiness and sanctification, without great sacrifice, and without a fervent prayer life, many will be so wounded. The evil spirit will answer, *"Jesus I know, Paul I know, but who are you?"*

It would do us well to be admonished by the great Apostle Paul, *"Finally, my brethren, be strong in the Lord and in the power of His might. Put on the whole armor of God, that you may be able to stand against the wiles of the devil. For we do not wrestle against flesh and blood, but against principalities, against powers, against the rulers of the darkness of this age, against spiritual hosts of wickedness in the heavenly places. Therefore, withstand in the evil day, and having done all, to stand. Stand, therefore, having girded your waist with truth, having put on the breastplate of righteousness, and having shod your feet with the preparation of the gospel of peace; above all, taking the shield of faith with which you will be able to quench all the fiery darts of the wicked one. And take the helmet of salvation, and the sword of the Spirit, which is the word of God; praying always with all prayer and supplication in the Spirit, being watchful to this end with all perseverance and supplication for all the saints."* (Ephesians 6:10-18)

" Finally, the more
who are trained to
fight and win, the
more God's light
will shine into this
dark world."
— *Larry Huggins*

ENDORSEMENT

By Larry Huggins, D.D

It's commonly accepted, a person is an expert if he or she has spent 10,000 hours or more concentrating on a single subject. Dick Bernal is an expert in spiritual warfare.

That's not just my opinion. It's an opinion held by many, contemporary, Christian leaders who have won spiritual battles because they applied the principles they learned from Pastor Dick Bernal, and they followed his example.

When Dick and his wife, Carla, were in Bible school, in Oklahoma, they attended FCF, a church I co-founded. After graduating from Bible school, they returned to California and launched Jubilee Christian Center, with a few family members and a handful of friends.

In 1982, when Jubilee was still a fledgling work, I invited Pastor Bernal to travel with me to India to help me conduct a miracle crusade. It was his introduction to miracle evangelism, and he took to it like a duck to water.

My team and I had organized five, concurrent crusades, in and around Guntur, India. The idea was to hold four satellite crusades, in four towns, and then our teams would come together for a big crusade in Guntur.

Dick may have thought he was going to be eased into the water. You know, first I would give him water wings, and then I would teach him how to dog paddle... No, I threw him into the deep end of the pool! This was his baptism into spiritual warfare.

Talk about culture shock: This wasn't sunny California, anymore. Dick was in a strange, noisy, dirty, demon-oppressed, third world environment like nothing he had ever seen or experienced before, with no time to decompress.

As soon as we arrived in Guntur, I paired him with his interpreter, put him in a car, and sent him to another city, by himself.

But Dick was a natural. As he preached his first crusade, the Holy Spirit moved, and miracles started happening. Large numbers of people were getting saved, healed, and set free.

Everything went smoothly... Until a powerful demon, manifesting through a woman, tried to disrupt the crusade. The powers of darkness challenged Dick's authority, and they were set on shutting down the crusade.

Although he had never experienced demon activity at this level, Dick intuitively knew what to do: he couldn't ignore it, and he couldn't back down, so he went on the offensive.

Before the eyes of thousands of cowering, idol-worshippers, Dick wrestled the demonized person to the ground, and with a thunderous voice of authority, he cast out the devil. The people were awestruck. That night, untold numbers of souls renounced the devil, forsook their idols, and made Jesus Lord of their lives.

Thus, Pastor Dick took his first, bold step on a long journey of spiritual warfare, on a trajectory that would pit him against bigger devils at higher levels.

Many of his battles became public spectacles. If fighting the forces of darkness wasn't enough, he was libeled by the hostile, secular press, and slandered by wrong-headed preachers.

However, Dick never quit. His mettle was forged in the crucible of fiery conflict. His battles were many, but his victories were more. People began viewing him as an Apostle of Spiritual Warfare, and they began seeking his help.

In the 5th Century BC, Sun Tzu wrote *The Art of War*, a treatise that enabled many of history's renowned generals, including America's great, General Douglas MacArthur, to defeat their enemies.

Dick Bernal has written a modern classic, *The Art of Spiritual Warfare*. It will help you win your personal, spiritual battles, and help you liberate your family, your city, and your nation.

This book should be in every Christian's library. We should buy it in large lots and pass it out to our friends and family. The more who are trained to fight and win, the more God's light will shine into this dark world.

Prepare yourself for war!

" And they overcame
him by the blood
of the Lamb and by
the word of their
testimony, and they
did not love their
lives to the death."

— *Revelation 12:11*

The Art of Spiritual Warfare

"Where you find an ocean you will find pirates."
(Old Malay proverb)

And war broke out in heaven: Michael and his angels fought with the dragon; and the dragon and his angels fought. (Revelation 12:7)

And they overcame him by the blood of the Lamb and by the word of their testimony, and they did not love their lives to the death. Therefore rejoice, O heavens, and you who dwell in them! Woe to the inhabitants of the earth and the sea! For the devil has come down to you, having great wrath, because he knows that he has a short time. (Revelation 12:11-12)

FAIT ACCOMPLI

I was born in October of 1944, during World War II. As a child, I had no idea of the grave events happening in my world — the battles, the victories, the losses, the death, and the struggles. The Korean Conflict was my introduction to war.

When I was a kid, I loved the movies. I especially loved the Saturday afternoon matinees. Before the cartoons and the feature film, they showed a clip called Movietone News. It was in black and white, of course.

Back then, the war in Korea dominated the newsreel shorts that we had to watch before we could see our favorite action heroes, Roy Rodgers or Flash Gordon on the silver screen.

I grew up in a rural setting with lots of kids to play with. Whenever a bunch of us got together we usually played cowboys and Indians, or war.

In February 1977, I was born again. However, I wasn't aware that another war was raging in the heavens — an invisible war started by Lucifer, whose army is comprised of one-third of the host of heaven who were drawn into spiritual rebellion by the tail of the Old Dragon.

It didn't take long for this new convert to realize I was not just saved but recruited into an army of believers, soldiers, and worshipping-warriors! As Matthew Henry said, "The Christian life is a life of war."

After seven decades of life, nearly half of that spent pastoring a local church and traveling the world preaching, I've learned some important things about overcoming the powers of darkness. My prayer is this book will help and in your journey of faith.

"The Christian life is a life of war."

— Matthew Henry

HOLY BIBLE

" I will build
My church,
and the gates
of Hades shall
not prevail
against it."

— *Revelation 12:11*

CHAPTER 1

The Gates of Hell

When Jesus came into the region of Caesarea Philipi, He asked His disciples, saying, "Who do men say that I, the Son of Man, am?" So they said, "Some say John the Baptist, some Elijah, and others Jeremiah or one of the prophets." He said to them, "But who do you say that I am?" Simon Peter answered and said, "You are the Christ, the Son of the living God." Jesus answered and said to him, "Blessed are you, Simon Bar-Jonah, for flesh and blood has not revealed this to you, but My Father who is in heaven. And I also say to you that you are Peter, and on this rock I will build My church, and the gates of Hades shall not prevail against it. And I will give you the keys of the kingdom of heaven, and whatever you bind on earth will be bound in heaven, and whatever you loose on earth will be loosed in heaven." Then He commanded His disciples that they should tell no one that He was Jesus the Christ. (Matthew 16:13-20)

Toward the end of our Lord's three plus years of ministry, He took His disciples to a very strange place at the very northern border of Israel, at what today is called Lebanon. There, was Caesarea Philippi, named after Caesar Augustus, and Herod's son, Philip. It's Arabic name was Banias, but because there is no "p" in the Arabic alphabet, it was by others called "Panais" named after the worship of the half-man, half-goat, flute playing god of the ancient greeks, Pan.

Pan was the god of the forests, fertility, music, watcher over shepherds and sheep, and a few other things. This is where Peter Pan came from. Author, J.M. Barrie created Peter Pan in the very early 1900's as a mischevious lad from Never Neverland who took kids away from parents to a place of fantasy.

Caesarea Philipi was no place for devout Jews. It was, and still is, a beautiful spot nestled in the foothills at the base of Mount Hermon, about twenty-five miles north of the Sea of Galilee.

It was a very popular place of worship for pagan Romans and Greeks during the time of Christ. Three temples were built there. One for Caesar, one for Pan, and the other for Zeus, called the god of gods by the ancients.

Why, toward the end of His time with the disciples would Jesus take them to such a pagan stronghold? Perhaps the most unclean area in all of Israel?

A few years back, on one of our Holy Land Tours, we visited Caesarea Philippi, and I was surprised to find the literal gate of hell; a cave, with a beautiful spring, fed by the head waters of the River Jordan, receiving its source from melting snow high upon Mount Hermon.

It was told that this cave was referred to as the gate to hell or the gate of hell, and the custom was for people to offer sacrifices to Pan by throwing goats or other objects into the cave-spring, and if the object floated down the river, they believed Pan was pleased. If the object sank (into hell), Pan was not pleased.

So, there stood Jesus with his twelve disciples in full view of all this demonic, carnal, worldly imagery, and He made this profound statement:

> *And I also say to you that you are Peter, and on this rock I will build My church, and the gates of Hades shall not prevail against it. And I will give you the keys of the kingdom of heaven, and whatever you bind on earth will be bound in heaven, and whatever you loose on earth will be loosed in heaven. (Matthew 16:18-19)*

Catch this as we begin our journey into the Art of Spiritual Warfare! These three temples represent worldly powers and governments (Temple of Caesar); the middle temple, the kingdom of satan and demons (Temple of Pan), and then the one erected to Zeus, the god of gods, representing all false religions past, present, and future (Temple of Zeus).

Jesus said, "upon this rock I will build my church". If you ever visit this region, or see a photo of it, you will notice the temples, and the gate of hell, are all at the bottom of a huge rock cliff.

What was He saying? He was saying, "my church, my kingdom" will be the one on top, overpowering all the world's governments, satan's kingdom, and false worship. The most powerful force the world will ever see is the united Body of Christ following our leader, our Lord Jesus, into victory!

Welcome to the war!

" Peace is the beauty
of life. It is sunshine,
it is the smile of a
child, the togetherness
of a family, it is the
advancement of a man,
the victory of a just
cause, the triumph
of truth."

— *Menachem Begin*

" Accept the challenges
so that you can feel the
exhilaration of victory."

— *General George Patton*

CHAPTER 2

A Kindergarten Lesson

The most exciting day of my young life was the first day of kindergarten. I was so excited I barely slept the night before. My two older sisters, Judy and Juanita, were already in school. I was envious when they got to board that big yellow school bus right in front of our house. Now, I was finally getting my chance to hop on board with all the other neighborhood kids and start my new adventure.

I had visited the school campus before because of the plays and activities my sisters were involved in. It was an old Navy compound left over from World War II that was redesigned as an elementary school for grades K-8.

Mom or Grandma would sit with me as I watched my sisters. I tried to imagine myself actually there in a new world called Freedom Elementary School.

The day finally came that I was part of it, and was I nervous! There were upper-class boys and girls on the bus, twelve and thirteen-year-old eighth graders from our neighborhood. I remember trying not to make eye contact with them fearing taunting or worse.

When we pulled into the bus parking lot, our teacher met the bus and instructed us to follow her to our new classroom. One girl on the bus I knew was also a first-timer.

Over twenty-five kids filled little desks. Parents and grandparents showed up to support their wide-eyed sons and daughters. My Grandmother was in the crowd, but I was more interested in sizing up the kids I had never met.

After formalities, the adults left and we sat and listened to Miss Tyman go over the day's schedule. Our first recess came quickly. Not knowing any of the boys, I gravitated toward Sandra Blue, my neighbor, and friend.

All of a sudden, out of nowhere, a kid named Kenny Phillips came up and punched me in the nose. I fell down, bleeding and crying. Kenny was the smallest kid in class. His older brothers had told him, "Pick out the tallest boy and punch him to let everyone know how tough you are."

Unfortunately, I was the tallest.

Of course, our teacher called our parents. Kenny got in trouble and I got pampered.

Kenny ended up being one of my best friends throughout grammar school. He never grew much, and every year he would plead with me, "Dick, please don't hit me back."

Kenny was raised by the Phillips clan, by a tough army veteran Dad, and a bunch of rough and tumble brothers. He had to learn how to fight just to survive at home.

Me, I was raised by four women. Even the girl across the street, Eileen, who was only one year older than I, and a tomboy, could out run, out wrestle, and out everything me.

It didn't take long for me to figure out that I had better learn to defend myself quickly or I would be the school's punching bag.

The next boy, Gary, who picked a fight with me, was sorry he did. Yep, I whipped him good, and then I was in my own trouble with Miss Tyman, Mom, and Grandma. But I smiled to myself through my punishment.

Word got out, don't mess with Dickie.

Gary also became a long time buddy.

As I entered my late teen years and early twenties I loved sports, working out, and teaching a Korean brand of Karate.

I took boxing lessons in college and I got into a few scraps along the way.

Not being a churchman, I had no qualms about living on the edge. I never looked for a fight, but I never backed away from one.

Then, at the age of thirty-two, I found Christ, and my life was changed forever. I began to attend church. Everyone was so nice, meek and mild. There were more women than men that attended, I noticed.

The music was soft and serene. The Pastor, a Christian his whole life, had a sweet smile and nice stories about his early days in Sunday school and seminary. Man, that was not the crowd I was used to, but I was in — I was all in!

The sermons were basically about trying to develop the fruit of the spirit, teaching us to be nice to one another, turn the other cheek, resist temptation, and look for the coming of the Lord, daily.

There's nothing wrong with any of that, but no one mentioned Satan, demons, spiritual warfare, or one's authority as a believer. There was no laying on of hands, no prayers for the sick, or any talk of the gifts of Spirit.

My dilemma was that, as I began to read the Bible for myself, and I saw power ministry in the first-century church, the things I read stirred me up and got me excited about one's potential in Christ.

Carla and I decided we needed more than our church offered. I was and still am grateful for my first year there, but my soul was hungry for more. My life changed again on October 8, 1978, when I was baptized in the Holy Spirit.

The next morning, I had a visitation in my little Toyota work truck around 5:00 a.m. on my way to Sacramento, California for work. To this day I'm not sure if an angel, Christ, or who manifested in my truck, but it got my attention for sure. An audible voice called me to serve God for the rest of my life, and a presence sat next to me. Did I imagine it? Maybe, but it was so real I will never forget it.

Two years later, Carla and I birthed Jubilee Christian Center in November of 1980. Little did I know the battle that lay ahead for us. The San Francisco Bay Area is one of Satan's strongholds. It has a legendary antichrist spirit and various principalities that cast a dark cloud over the area's eight million people.

For a while, it was like my first days in kindergarten. I was so lost in the newness, and fun, and freedom of my new school that I was unprepared for the wiles of the other kids. However, I became spiritually tough, quickly.

After thirty-seven years of successfully leading a congregation in the heart of the Silicon Valley, I have many victorious stories of spiritual battles, how we penetrated Babylon and won.

" You have to expect spiritual warfare whenever you stand up for righteousness or call attention to basic values."

— *Thomas Kinkade*

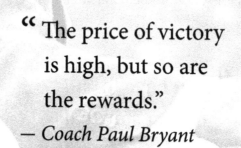

" The price of victory
is high, but so are
the rewards."
— *Coach Paul Bryant*

CHAPTER 3

War of the Worlds

Fight the good fight of faith, lay hold on eternal life, to which you were also called and have confessed the good confession in the presence of many witnesses. (1 Timothy 6:12)

There are three arenas of conflict for the believer: (1) the world, (2) the flesh, and of course, (3) the devil.

The world (*GK-kosmos*) speaks of systems, governments, lifestyles, religions, philosophies, culture, traditions, and the sort.

The word secular means unspiritual or non-religious. It also means temporal.

We are in a secular world, but not *of* it. For example, I'm foremost a Christian, who happens to be an American, a Californian, and a resident of San Jose, California. I'm a white male with Hispanic forefathers and English and Irish foremothers. But, again, all that said, I'm a citizen of heaven first.

Politically, I'm a registered lamb-lion party member. I vote, yes, according to my faith and Judeo-Christian beliefs. I honor and pray for authorities, but I worship my King.

Watching the world going to hell in a hand-basket doesn't scare me nor dishearten me. I believe the prophecy of Isaiah is upon us:

> *Arise, shine; For your light has come! And the glory of the Lord is risen upon you. For behold, the darkness shall cover the earth, and deep darkness the people; But the Lord will arise over you, And His glory will be seen upon you.*

> *The Gentiles shall come to your light, And kings to the brightness of your rising. Lift up your eyes all around, and see: They all gather together, they come to you; Your sons shall come from afar, and your daughters shall be nursed at your side. Then you shall see and become radiant, and your heart shall swell with joy; because the abundance of the sea shall be turned to you, the wealth of the Gentiles shall come to you. (Isaiah 60:1-5)*

If love and light are two of our chief weapons of warfare, then the hate and darkness around us must bow their knees to the power of Christ our Lord. It's our time to rise and shine!

John wrote about God's light in his gospel:

> *In the beginning was the Word, and the Word was with God, and the Word was God. He was in the beginning with God. All things were made through Him, and without Him nothing was made that was made. In Him was life, and the life was the light of men. And the light shines in the darkness, and the darkness did not comprehend it. (John 1:1-5)*

Darkness tried, but could not conquer the light of Jesus. When fighting an invisible foe, we need powerful weapons:

> *For though we walk in the flesh, we do not war according to the flesh. For the weapons of our warfare are not carnal but mighty in God for pulling down strongholds, casting down arguments and every high thing that exalts itself against the knowledge of God, bringing every thought into captivity to the obedience of Christ, and being ready to punish all disobedience when your obedience is fulfilled. (2 Corinthians 10:3-6)*

Paul to the Ephesians:

> *For we do not wrestle against flesh and blood, but against principalities, against powers, against the rulers of the darkness of this age, against spiritual hosts of wickedness in the heavenly places. Therefore take up the whole armor of God, that you may be able to withstand in the evil day, and having done all, to stand. (Ephesians 6:12-13)*

People are not our biggest problem. I know this is hard to believe, seeing that sometimes folks act like the devil himself. But Paul tells the church that we don't wrestle or struggle with flesh and blood. We must focus the crosshairs of our spiritual weapons upon the real enemy, upon Satanic principalities, and powers, and evil rulers of this age that occupy the atmosphere from which the army of evil operates.

Lucifer's minions are organized. I believe he learned how

to organize his army by watching how God managed the heavenly host.

A side note: It's one thing to cast out an unclean demon, yet quite another to try to pull down a strong territorial prince over a region. Trust me, I know. (More on this later in the book!)

Jesus commissioned the church to "Go into all the world." But, first, He made the early saints wait for the power of the Holy Spirit:

> *And being assembled together with them, He commanded them not to depart from Jerusalem, but to wait for the Promise of the Father, "which," He said, "you have heard from Me; for John truly baptized with water, but you shall be baptized with the Holy Spirit not many days from now." Therefore, when they had come together, they asked Him, saying, "Lord, will You at this time restore the kingdom to Israel?" And He said to them, "It is not for you to know times or seasons which the Father has put in His own authority. But you shall receive power when the Holy Spirit has come upon you; and you shall be witnesses to Me in Jerusalem, and in all Judea and Samaria, and to the end of the earth. (Acts 1:4-8)*

Christ, knowing the resistance the church would face, told the early church to wait for "Power from on high" — the power to preach, to heal, to cast out devils, to do signs and wonders, and to build churches.

One of my favorite parts of the Book of Acts has to do with Paul's amazing ministry in Ephesus. Ephesus, you may know, was a major city of great importance. It was cultured and fast-paced, a city of commerce, art, and sports; but it was also the center of Diana worship.

Paul found a handful of new converts who had received the baptism of John the Baptist — a baptism of repentance, not of fire. So, Paul educates them, and he lays his hands on them, and pow! Here comes the power, just like on the day of Pentecost!

> *And it happened, while Apollos was at Corinth, that Paul, having passed through the upper regions, came to Ephesus. And finding some disciples he said to them, "Did you receive the Holy Spirit when you believed?"*
>
> *So they said to him, "We have not so much as heard whether there is a Holy Spirit." And he said to them, "Into what then were you baptized?" So they said, "Into John's baptism." Then Paul said, "John indeed baptized with a baptism of repentance, saying to the people that they should believe on Him who would come after him, that is, on Christ Jesus." When they heard this, they were baptized in the name of the Lord Jesus. And when Paul had laid hands on them, the Holy Spirit came upon them, and they spoke with tongues and prophesied. Now the men were about twelve in all. (Acts 19:1-7)*

San Francisco reminds me of ancient Ephesus, a major port-trade city. Ephesus was vibrant, exciting, and beautiful, yet spiritually dark, because Diana held Ephesus in her grip. The ruling principality over San Francisco, likewise, has produced a culture and stronghold which loudly says NO to the Gospel of Christ.

Years ago, I wrote in my book, *Storming Hell's Brazen Gates,* an interesting fact about the Great Seal of the State of California. The seal depicts an image of Minerva, the Roman goddess of wisdom, art, and war. The Greeks called her Athena. It's the same demon principality as the daughter of Jupiter/Zeus. Minerva, a woman-warrior, dressed in a man's armor, stands overlooking the San Francisco Bay and the Golden Gate Straights.

Also, on the seal of California, is a grizzly bear at the feet of Minerva. Interestingly, according to the architect of our state's seal, the grizzly bear was meant to represent strength and independence. The problem is, there are no more grizzly bears in California. They were killed off years ago.

If you want to know the name of the principality over San Francisco, just look at the state's seal. Minerva has a stronghold over this beautiful City by the Bay that is known worldwide as a city of culture, tolerance, revelry, far left politics, and a sanctuary city. Today, San Francisco is one of the most anti-Christ, anti-Bible, anti-church (and anti-preacher) cities in the world.

When the 1906 earthquake leveled San Francisco, did it bring revival? No! The people of the city went right back to business as usual. The Barbary Coast, also known as Bagdad by the

Bay, was rebuilt with even more banks, brothels, saloons, and places to revel.

Los Angeles, on the other hand, is a different story. The Azusa Street Revival broke out just days after the San Andreas earthquake leveled San Francisco. Why? Many Christian leaders in Los Angeles believed the 1906 earthquake was a result of God's judgment on San Francisco, and that Los Angeles might be next.

Over one hundred years later, mega-churches can be found all over the Los Angeles area, but not in San Francisco — not even close. Recently, however, there have been some encouraging signs of a few San Francisco churches seeing growth, especially among young people. For the most part, we see a graveyard of past attempts to save our city.

Today, San Francisco is referred to as the Gateway City. The Golden Gate Bridge, which spans the Golden Gate Straights, is the principal landmark. That's important. We will take a look at the importance of gates from a biblical point of view. But before we do, will you join your faith with ours and agree that the ruling principality will come down?

Come down, Minerva! Comedown, in Jesus name!

"The gates of hell
are locked from
the inside…"
— *C.S. Lewis*

CHAPTER 4

Gates

He said to them, "But who do you say that I am?" Simon Peter answered and said, "You are the Christ, the Son of the living God." Jesus answered and said to him, "Blessed are you, Simon Bar-Jonah, for flesh and blood has not revealed this to you, but My Father who is in heaven. And I also say to you that you are Peter, and on this rock I will build My church, and the gates of Hades shall not prevail against it. (Matthew 16:15-19)

Then the Angel of the Lord called to Abraham a second time out of heaven, and said: "By Myself I have sworn, says the Lord, because you have done this thing, and have not withheld your son, your only son — blessing I will bless you, and multiplying I will multiply your descendants as the stars of the heaven and as the sand which is on the seashore; and your descendants shall possess the gate of their enemies. In your seed all the nations of the earth shall be blessed, because you have obeyed My voice." (Genesis 22:15-18)

Then Jacob awoke from his sleep and said, "Surely the Lord is in this place, and I did not know it." And he was afraid and said, "How awesome is this place! This is none other than the house of God, and this is the gate of heaven!" (Genesis 28:16-17)

Every day we pass through doors or gates as we go about our business. They're a part of life we take for granted. My house has a front door, garage door, sliding glass doors leading to the backyard, and two exterior gates on either side of my home. Some neighborhoods have guard gates. Airlines, stadiums, government complexes, even national and state parks have gates.

To understand spiritual warfare one must have a revelation of *gates* from a biblical perspective: gates of hell, gates of our enemies, and the gate of heaven. Here's a modern definition of gate: *a hinged barrier used to close an opening in a wall, fence, or hedge.* In the days the Bible was written the word gate had a much more profound meaning.

In Hebrew, the word for gate is *shaar: an opening; that which encloses a wall or fortified compound for safety concerns.* The Greeks used the word *poolay,* meaning, *a passage that can either lead to life or destruction.* Got to love the Greeks! So poetic and dramatic. I love their definition.

The gates of ancient cities were key gathering places of important people. Civic and military plans as well as business dealings were often made at the gate of a city. So, in antiquity, the city gate spoke of power and authority. When Jesus told

Peter, "...the gates of hell will not prevail against the church," He was likening hell to a city, metaphorically. This shouldn't surprise us because Christ called His body a city set on a hill.

> *By faith Abraham obeyed when he was called to go out to the place which he would receive as an inheritance. And he went out, not knowing where he was going. By faith he dwelt in the land of promise as in a foreign country, dwelling in tents with Isaac and Jacob, the heirs with him of the same promise; for he waited for the city which has foundations, whose builder and maker is God. (Hebrews 11:8-10)*

In the book of Revelation, John saw the holy city, New Jerusalem, a city foursquare, coming down from heaven. In contrast, picture hell as a city — a dark, foreboding, evil city full of principalities, rulers of darkness, and wicked spirits as its citizens!

The Bible is the original tale of two cities at war. Even the Greek word for city, *polis*, speaks of a place of struggle. The Hebrew word for city, *awyar*, literally means, *to awake and watch; a fortified place where eyes are open.*

We see God working today the same as he did in Biblical days, appointing men and women (pastors, churches, ministries) in cities to establish God's rule in the earth. He does with us as he did with Jeremiah:

> *Then the Lord put forth His hand and touched my mouth, and the Lord said to me: "Behold, I have put My words in your mouth. See, I have this day set you over*

the nations and over the kingdoms, To root out and to
pull down, To destroy and to throw down, To build and
to plant." Moreover the word of the Lord came to me,
saying, "Jeremiah, what do you see?" And I said, "I see
a branch of an almond tree." (Jeremiah 1:9-12)

The almond tree is a symbol of God's prophetic decree. The
almond tree is the first tree to flower in the spring. Hence,
it's called the *announcing* tree! I lived in almond country
for a few years, in Butte County, Northern California. The
Almond trees were the first to bud and let us all know spring
was coming — a new season was upon us.

Cities were often named for the physical attributes observed
by man when discovering and settling lands. For example,
the city of Luz was named for the abundance of almond trees
found in that city. Luz means, *where there are almond trees.*
Jacob changed the name of Luz to Bethel, meaning *house of*
God, prophetically announcing the greatest gate of all — the
Gate of Heaven.

And he called the name of that place Bethel; but
the name of that city had been Luz previously.
(Genesis 28:19)

Bethel is our city! It's the city of God, and we sit at the gates
of Bethel in our position of safety and authority. The local
church, one who knows her authority in Christ, where God's
presence is wanted, welcomed, and worshipped, is a gate of
blessing under an open heaven bringing life, and joy, and
peace into a city!

" Far better is it to
dare mighty things,
to win glorious
triumphs, even
though checkered
by failure…
than to rank with
those poor spirits
who neither enjoy
nor suffer much,
because they live
in a gray twilight
that knows not
victory nor defeat."
— *Theodore Roosevelt*

" Victory is always
possible for the
person who refuses
to stop fighting."

— *Napaleon Hill*

CHAPTER 5

The Why Factor

Now these are the nations which the Lord left, that He might test Israel by them, that is, all who had not known any of the wars in Canaan [this was only so that the generations of the children of Israel might be taught to know war, at least those who had not formerly known it]. (Judges 3:1-2)

Since our first Sunday way back in November 1980, with a handful of people, I've been asked on a regular basis, "Why Pastor, why? Why is this happening to me or to us? I'm a good Christian, I try my best, I support God's work. So why Pastor?"

Somehow many well-meaning precious people have the misconception being born-again, attending church on a regular basis, even tithing should exempt them from troubles. Even a casual glance at the scriptures will dispel that fantasy. Remember the movie, *Bubbleboy*, a story about a young man who had an autoimmune disease where he had to live in a plastic bubble just to survive. Spiritually there is no such thing as a Christian bubble to exempt us from life and all its challenges.

The air is infested with uncountable demons. The world is anti-Christ, and our flesh is a rebel with a cause. Matthew Henry wrote, "The Christian life is a life of spiritual warfare." The Key for us is, do we know how to fight the good *fight of faith* or let whatever will be, will be, like so many fatalistic religions and philosophies? How important is it to learn how to war? What are warfare prayers? How do we know when to pick a fight and with who?

Then Joshua rose early in the morning; and they set out from Acacia Grove and came to the Jordan, he and all the children of Israel, and lodged there before they crossed over. So it was, after three days, that the officers went through the camp; and they commanded the people, saying, "When you see the ark of the covenant of the Lord your God, and the priests, the Levites, bearing it, then you shall set out from your place and go after it. Yet there shall be a space between you and it, about two thousand cubits by measure. Do not come near it, that you may know the way by which you must go, for you have not passed this way before." And Joshua said to the people, "Sanctify yourselves, for tomorrow the Lord will do wonders among you." Then Joshua spoke to the priests, saying, "Take up the ark of the covenant and cross over before the people." So they took up the ark of the covenant and went before the people. And the Lord said to Joshua, "This day I will begin to exalt you in the sight of all Israel, that they may know that, as I was with Moses, so I will be with you. You shall command the priests who bear the ark of the covenant, saying, 'When you have come to the edge of the water of the Jordan, you shall stand in the Jordan.'" So Joshua said to the children of Israel, "Come here, and hear the words of the Lord your God." And Joshua said, "By this you shall know that the living God isamong you, and that He will without fail drive out from before you the Canaanites and the Hittites and the Hivites and the Perizzites and the Girgashites and the Amorites and the Jebusites: Behold, the ark of the covenant of the Lord of all the earth is crossing over before you into the Jordan." (Joshua 3:1-11)

Christians want to live as if Satan is defeated and harmless, and demons are unemployed, and it's nothing but smooth sailing from Calvary to His return. No, Walt Disney created Fantasyland, not Jesus Christ. There is no fairy dust or magic wand that will turn a frog into a Prince. Jesus could have said, "I'm finished, you're not. Pick up your cross and follow me."

Okay, let me address this problem. At the heart of Theodicy is an apparent contradiction. Yes, at the cross satan was legally defeated, but it's the church and believers who *vitalize the legal.* We are to enforce and remind satan and his, who the real victors are. The big picture is as simple as three c's: the Cosmic Conflict, the Cross, and the Church! This existential problem of reconciling these two truths is crystal clear to me.

Jesus ministered — we minister; He was loved and hated — we are loved and hated; Satan tempted Him — likewise we are tempted; A friend betrayed Him — we've been betrayed; He was crucified — so must we crucify our flesh; He went to hell — we, at times, go through hell; He rose from the dead — we are born again; He now is seated at the right hand of the Father — we are also seated in heavenly places.

Jesus did not die so we would never have challenges. He gave us power and authority to overcome the evil one and by his Holy Spirit, teaching us how to push back the powers of darkness and claim souls, even cities for Christ.

> *Though He was a Son, yet He learned obedience by the things which He suffered. And having been perfected, He became the author of eternal salvation to all who obey Him. (Hebrews 5:8-9)*

If obedience and perfection came to our Lord through tests, trials, and tribulations, why should we be surprised or shocked when life happens. How much would we pray, really, if we never had challenges?

We can't go to *something* until we go *through something*. David had to go through Goliath, to get to the throne. To truly be an overcomer, we have to have stuff to come over. James, the brother of Jesus, a man who did not believe in his own brother until after the resurrection, wrote:

> *James, a bondservant of God and of the Lord Jesus Christ, To the twelve tribes which are scattered abroad: Greetings. My brethren, count it all joy when you fall into various trials, knowing that the testing of your faith produces patience. But let patience have its perfect work, that you may be perfect and complete, lacking nothing. If any of you lacks wisdom, let him ask of God, who*

gives to all liberally and without reproach, and it will be given to him. But let him ask in faith, with no doubting, for he who doubts is like a wave of the sea driven and tossed by the wind. For let not that man suppose that he will receive from the Lord; he is a double-minded man, unstable in all his ways. (James 1-8)

How many people "Count it all joy" when all hell is breaking loose? James was looking past the problems to the product. The ones counting hardships as joy and laughing in the face of the enemy are the believers who patiently grow stronger and wiser with each victory.

Back in 1980, when Carla and I started Jubilee here in the Bay Area, an area famous for innovations and export of ideas, lifestyles, and electronic gadgets, we didn't know the nature of the beast that we challenged.

The principality over this region, one of Satan's chief seats, was not used to being confronted publically. In my naivety and zeal, freshly coming out of Rhema Bible Training Center, I made several near-fatal mistakes.

Moving up quickly in faith and not having a Holy Ghost strategy of warfare, I tried single-handedly to pull him down. That was a huge mistake, and boy did I pay for it! The big miracle is, I'm still here, still married, still healthy, and still in the arena of battle.

I hope this book will help some Pastors and Leaders avoid some of the pitfalls that nearly took me out. I no longer ask, "Why?" I pray, "How?"

" Be ashamed to
die until you have
won some victory
for humanity."
— *Horace Mann*

CHAPTER 6

What's In Your Hand?

Then Moses answered and said, "But suppose they will not believe me or listen to my voice; suppose they say, 'The Lord has not appeared to you.'" So the Lord said to him, "What is that in your hand?" He said, "A rod." And He said, "Cast it on the ground." So he cast it on the ground, and it became a serpent; and Moses fled from it. Then the Lord said to Moses, "Reach out your hand and take it by the tail" (and he reached out his hand and caught it, and it became a rod in his hand), "that they may believe that the Lord God of their fathers, the God of Abraham, the God of Isaac, and the God of Jacob, has appeared to you." (Exodus 4:1-5)

Little did Moses know, that old piece of dead wood carved into a rod (staff) would end up being a mighty weapon against darkness. Jesus' first miracle was turning water into wine. Moses' first miracle, after the rod became a viper, was turning water into blood.

Later, in the wilderness, Moses raised his rod and the Red Sea parted. Also, water came from a rock when he struck with his rod. Amazing! So, I ask what's in your hand? What gift do you have to offer God?

I was a steelworker. I had tools in my hand to build structures of iron and concrete. Now, I have tools for building the Kingdom, the church, and lives.

David used a slingshot. Samson used the jawbone of an ass. Elijah and Elisha, used a mantle. Jesus used a young boy's loaves and fishes. God used the widow's two mites. He used the fishermen's nets. Paul had tent-making tools, and Jesus had nails.

What's in your hand that, given to God, can be a mighty weapon against the kingdom of hell? Each of us has something to give to God. We are uniquely gifted. It seems we admire everyone else's gift, but we don't recognize our own. We think, "If only I could be more like that." No! You should just be you. You're good at something. What is your greatest gift to the Kingdom of God?

> Blessed be the Lord my Rock, who trains my hands for war, and my fingers for battle. (Psalms 144:1)

If you take the lessons of this book to heart, and follow the examples of our heroes of faith, you will be equipped to fight and win on every score. What's in your hand? Your heart? Your mouth? A miracle is waiting to be released!

CHAPTER 7

Gate of Heaven

For decades, I've been teaching on how to open heaven or how to keep the heavens open over you, your family, your church, and someday your city, state, region, and even your nation.

I love these portions of John's Gospel and Revelation:

Philip found Nathanael and said to him, "We have found Him of whom Moses in the law, and also the prophets, wrote—Jesus of Nazareth, the son of Joseph." And Nathanael said to him, "Can anything good come out of Nazareth?" Philip said to him, "Come and see." Jesus saw Nathanael coming toward Him, and said of him, "Behold, an Israelite indeed, in whom is no deceit!" Nathanael said to Him, "How do You know me?" Jesus answered and said to him, "Before Philip called you, when you were under the fig tree, I saw you." Nathanael answered and said to Him, "Rabbi, You are the Son of God! You are the King of Israel!" Jesus answered and said to him, "Because I said to you, 'I saw you under the fig tree,' do you believe? You will see greater things than these." And He said to him, "Most assuredly, I say to

you, hereafter you shall see heaven open, and the angels of God ascending and descending upon the Son of Man."
(John 1:45-51)

After these things I looked, and behold, a door standing open in heaven. And the first voice which I heard was like a trumpet speaking with me, saying, "Come up here, and I will show you things which must take place after this." Immediately I was in the Spirit; and behold, a throne set in heaven, and One sat on the throne."
(Revelation 4:1-2)

Revelation brings elevation! Because of our Lord's obedience to His Father God, Jesus had an open heaven wherever he went, even in a region where the heavens were brass, and the earth was iron.

And your heavens which are over your head shall be bronze, and the earth which is under you shall be iron. The Lord will change the rain of your land to powder and dust; from the heaven it shall come down on you until you are destroyed. (Deuteronomy 28:23-24)

Rome had taken ownership of Israel years before Jesus was born. In the book of Malachi, God tried to protect Israel from this, but his plan fell on deaf ears. There was no prophetic word or revival for 400 years until John the Baptist. Then Christ came on the scene. Then, all of a sudden, there was an opening in the brazen skies.

This blessing of an open heaven got Satan's attention. There was a breach in his demonic barricade.

The first place we see this is in Genesis. Jacob is fleeing from his brother, Esau's, fury, and is headed to Haran in Syria to start a new life.

> *Now Jacob went out from Beersheba and went toward Haran. So he came to a certain place and stayed there all night because the sun had set. And he took one of the stones of that place and put it at his head, and he lay down in that place to sleep. Then he dreamed, and behold, a ladder was set up on the earth, and its top reached to heaven; and there the angels of God were ascending and descending on it. And behold, the Lord stood above it and said: "I am the Lord God of Abraham your father and the God of Isaac; the land on which you lie I will give to you and your descendants. Also your descendants shall be as the dust of the earth; you shall spread abroad to the west and the east, to the north and the south; and in you and in your seed all the families of the earth shall be blessed. Behold, I am with you and will keep you wherever you go, and will bring you back to this land; for I will not leave you until I have done what I have spoken to you." (Genesis 28:10-15)*

Jacob experienced an open heaven. How do we know if there is an open heaven over our lives, our church? One identifying factor is when the prophetic voice is active and ongoing! One thing we've had at Jubilee ever since 1980, is the manifestation of the spirit of prophecy. We believe in giving people a word in due season. One rhema word from God can be more life-changing than a thousand sermons.

Every major move in my life came from a right now, ready, rhema, rudder word!

An old preacher friend told me once, "Watch for the pointing that leads to the anointing." What did he mean by that? Well, God pointed Noah to "Build an ark." Abraham pointed Lot to "Go!" An Angel pointed to Gideon saying, "O mighty man of valor." Samuel pointed to David saying, "He's the one." The king pointed to Esther saying, "Come here." John the Baptist pointed people to Jesus to "Follow Him." Jesus pointed the twelve to "Follow Me."

Someone asked me during a Christian television station interview, "Dick, in your opinion, what's good church?"

I answered, "It's when we are all challenged to do something we've never done before for God, resulting in transformed lives."

We have been given power and authority to open or close, bind or loose, declare or decree the will and wisdom of God.

To me, who am less than the least of all the saints, this grace was given, that I should preach among the Gentiles the unsearchable riches of Christ, and to make all see what is the fellowship of the mystery, which from the beginning of the ages has been hidden in God who created all things through Jesus Christ; to the intent that now the manifold wisdom of God might be made known by the church to the principalities and powers in the heavenly places, according to the eternal purpose which He accomplished in Christ Jesus our Lord, in whom we have boldness and access with confidence through faith in Him." (Ephesians 3:8-12)

It's no longer a secret: God's original intent, even His manifold wisdom, is now in the stewardship of the church, and it's our duty and honor to teach good angels and fallen angels the role of the church and the purpose and intent of God throughout the ages.

What can we teach righteous angels? Well, one thing is, we believe without seeing. Angels see God every day. They live in heaven. They don't hurt, struggle, cry, suffer loss, go through a divorce, death, sickness, or lack. Yet, for us humans, through all things, and in all things, we still worship. We still sing. We still come to church. We still tithe, shout, and raise our hands to a God we've never seen, and we believe in a place we've never been to, called heaven. Angels must be in awe of our faith! Throughout all of that, demons try night and day to discourage us, tempt us, and destroy us. Nevertheless, we win, and they lose — it's got to drive them nuts!

Like most leaders, I've been attacked, sued, lied on, betrayed, stolen from, accused of, and taken advantage of. Yet, I'm still standing, still preaching, still loving people, still dreaming, still having visions, still smiling, and still believing. It's a fight, but it's a good fight!

Yet in all these things we are more than conquerors through Him who loved us. (Romans 8:37)

Here's my advice — don't even think about quitting. Remember the old saying, "Quitters never win, and winners never quit."

> *Submit yourselves therefore to God. Resist the devil, and he will flee from you. (James 4:7)*

Make up your mind to stay with the battle until the devil gives in. When he sees that you have no intention of quitting, he will cut his losses short and withdraw. However, don't let your guard down. You can be sure that sooner or later he will try again.

" Victory belongs
to the most
perservering"
— *Napolean Bonaparte*

CHAPTER 8

The Flesh!

Watch and pray, lest you enter into temptation. The spirit indeed is willing, but the flesh is weak. (Matthew 26:41)

That pretty much sums it up. The flesh is weak, so Jesus tells us to watch and pray.

The disciples were sleeping. No doubt, the rigors of the day wore them out. What about Jesus? Was he tired? Yes! However, He knew He Himself must watch and pray against temptation. He knew what was coming: soldiers, an arrest, a horrible beating, and a cruel death on the cross.

In Matthew's Gospel, we see the human side of our precious Lord. He had the will, but not the desire to suffer upon the cross:

He went away again the second time, and prayed, saying, O my Father, if this cup may not pass away from me, except I drink it, thy will be done. And he came and found them asleep again; for their eyes were heavy. And he left them, and went away again, and prayed the third time, saying the same words. (Matthew 26:42-44)

What I want to address here is this: as long as we are in this world we have a spirit, a soul, and a body. My body, and, at times, my mind can't keep up with my spirit.

Paul wrote to the the Saints in Rome:

> *I thank God through Jesus Christ our Lord. So then with the mind I myself serve the law of God; but with the flesh the law of sin. (Romans 7:25)*

I can attest that some of the poorest decisions I ever made came from weariness of body, not thinking it through, and not praying it out first. I would like to think I'm a pretty easygoing guy who hates strife and angry outbursts. Yet, if I'm tired and not sleeping, I can snap with the best turtles in the swamp.

Recently, I went through the perfect storm of battles: finances, personal ministry, marriage, health, people, and family. I nearly had a meltdown. After that, I was convinced that I needed to take a month or so off to pray, rest, fish, look at the ocean, catch a movie, and have some down time.

For over thirty years, I had never taken a time to rest. Why? Was I a workaholic? No. I love my calling. I love my church, my staff, and my members. Staying away was one of the hardest things I had ever done, but it was necessary.

A valuable lesson I learned during that time is when we aren't rested we start to lose touch with God's grace and compassion. Faith works best when we are at rest!

Therefore, since a promise remains of entering His rest, let us fear lest any of you seem to have come short of it. For indeed the gospel was preached to us as well as to them; but the word which they heard did not profit them, not being mixed with faith in those who heard it. For we who have believed do enter that rest, as He has said: "So I swore in My wrath, 'They shall not enter My rest,'" (Hebrews 4:1-3)

When I was a rookie pastor, in 1981, a visiting missionary, who was an elder statesman, took me to lunch and began mentoring me, which he continued to do until he died. "Dick, watch out for the Three F's – beasts that can destroy you and your ministry: lust for Fame, Females, and Finances can take you out."

Over the last thirty-seven years, I've seen way too many anointed men and women of God fall prey to the limelight or money or sexual indiscretions. I've seen many divorced families and torn apart churches go under because of the Three F's – beasts that must be tamed.

Where do wars and fights come from among you? Do they not come from your desires for pleasure that war in your members? You lust and do not have. You murder and covet and cannot obtain. You fight and war. Yet you do not have because you do not ask. You ask and do not receive, because you ask amiss, that you may spend it on your pleasures. Adulterers and adulteresses! Do you not know that friendship with the world is enmity with God? Whoever therefore wants to be a friend of the world makes himself an enemy of God. Or do you think that the Scripture says in vain, "The Spirit who dwells in us yearns jealously?" (James 4:1-5)

For thirty-two years I walked in the flesh. The fallen nature of man dominated my life. I believed in a God; even heaven, hell, the devil, angels — all of it — but it wasn't personal. I think we even had a big old white family Bible somewhere gathering dust, but it was never opened, much less studied. I respected the church, and I enjoyed Bible epics in the movie house, but they didn't affect my choices or lifestyle.

I say then: Walk in the Spirit, and you shall not fulfill the lust of the flesh. For the flesh lusts against the Spirit, and the Spirit against the flesh; and these are contrary to one another, so that you do not do the things that you wish. But if you are led by the Spirit, you are not under the law. (Galatians 5:16-18)

We, sinners, sin because of the law of sin that rules over our very being. Growing up in the '60's in the Bay Area didn't help. The party scene in San Francisco was too tempting to pass up. We lived for the day with no thought of tomorrow. I worked hard as an ironworker, basically to pay for a big weekend of revelry. I was good at sinning, had fun at it, and never saw a need to quit. Why stop having a ball, are you kidding me?

Oh sure, now and then I would confess to my friends that I needed to slow down because my life was getting out of control. But that didn't help me change my life.

It was usually thoughts of my dad that crept in that caused me to contemplate my own life. My dad died at fifty-six from a massive heart attack. He drank like a fish, smoked two packs of cigarettes a day, and took amphetamines to keep him awake so he could drive trucks from San Jose to Los Angeles three times a week.

Here I was in my late twenties, and if not careful, it seemed, I wouldn't make it to fifty-six. Those rare moments of clarity, however, didn't stop a thing. My flesh was in control, and I was on a highway to hell. This would all drastically change in the coming few years.

On my 30th birthday, I was in Ogden, Utah, building a warehouse. It was late October. A cold front moved in that day. I drove a borrowed pick up to the Mountains with a bottle of whiskey and a pack of cigarettes to ring in my thirtieth year.

As I lay on the hood of the pickup, I began looking back at my life. Not much to be proud of except for my son, Adam, who was ten and living with his mom and stepdad.

Sometimes alcohol helped ease the guilt and pain of failure, but not this night. It began to snow, but I didn't care. I drank my whiskey and took another drag on my cigarette. As I blew smoke circles towards the snowy sky, I decided to talk to God. "Hey, anyone up there? I could use some help."

For the first time, I began thinking of the future. Did I want another 30 years of this? Alone, just surviving paycheck to paycheck, with no real plan, no dreams? Did heaven answer?

No, not that night; but soon enough.

Six weeks later I met a little redheaded Baptist girl, Carla Fobroy. Like any good Baptist, she began witnessing to me about Jesus, and I listened.

Not long after we were married, the devil tried to kill her. That's when I accepted Christ. It was the best thing that ever happened to me. After I received Christ, I had to learn how to walk in the spirit. This learning path, of course, never ends as long as we are in this body, but continues with prayer, renewing of the mind, a good confession, attending church, and fellowship with the saints. What a wonderous life it is!

> *Therefore, if anyone is in Christ, he is a new creation; old things have passed away; behold, all things have become new. (2 Corinthians 5:17)*

" Victory has a thousand fathers, but defeat is an orphan."
— *John F. Kennedy*

CHAPTER 9

Authority

Go therefore and make disciples of all the nations, baptizing them in the name of the Father and of the Son and of the Holy Spirit, teaching them to observe all things that I have commanded you; and lo, I am with you always, even to the end of the age. Amen." (Matthew 28:19-20)

He who believes and is baptized will be saved; but he who does not believe will be condemned. And these signs will follow those who believe: In My name they will cast out demons; they will speak with new tongues; they will take up serpents; and if they drink anything deadly, it will by no means hurt them; they will lay hands on the sick, and they will recover." (Mark 16:16-18)

Then the seventy returned with joy, saying, "Lord, even the demons are subject to us in Your name." And He said to them, "I saw Satan fall like lightning from heaven. Behold, I give you the authority to trample on serpents and scorpions, and over all the power of the enemy, and nothing shall by any means hurt you. Nevertheless do not rejoice in this, that the spirits are subject to you, but rather rejoice because your names are written in heaven." (Luke 10:17-20)

As a new, born-again, spirit-filled convert the greatest revelation that hit my mind and spirit was that I have spiritual authority. The Greek word for authority is *exousia*, which speaks of privilege, capacity, competency, mastery, and control. We have the right, the power of attorney, to use the name of Jesus and His shed blood along with our personal testimony to overcome the evil one.

> *And they overcame him by the blood of the Lamb and by the word of their testimony, and they did not love their lives to the death. Therefore rejoice, O heavens, and you who dwell in them! Woe to the inhabitants of the earth and the sea! For the devil has come down to you, having great wrath, because he knows that he has a short time. (Revelations 12:11-12)*

It's apparent in these last of the last days, the devil is ratcheting up his attack. He knows the clock is ticking and his season is about up. Thank God for the name of Jesus, the power of His shed blood, and our story.

During my first mission trip to Guntur, India in 1982, with Pastor Huggins, I became fully cognizant of the need for these three weapons of our warfare: The name, the blood, and my testimony!

After I shared my sermon and personal testimony of what Christ did for me, thousands of Hindu men, women and children ran to the platform for help. It was overwhelming at first because I had never seen a crowd so hungry and passionate for God to bless them as I saw that night in India. God's healing and delivering power fell like a giant mantle from heaven, converting almost everyone to Christ that night.

One old blind man was healed and cried, "I can see, I can see!" Many other's limbs were straightened by the laying on of hands. It was awesome!

What I remember most was a young teenage girl who was demonized. At first, she looked normal. Her head was bowed and her eyes closed. Then, all of a sudden, she fell to the ground and turned into a serpent! A serpent spirit had possessed her. She slithered around, hissing, tongue darting in and out like a snake. The snake-girl stared at me for a few seconds.

My interpreters said, "Reverend Dick, demons."

I thought, *Duh! No kidding?*

It was my first experience at seeing how powerful the name of Jesus and pleading His blood is. It drove that snake devil crazy.

I kept yelling, "In the name of Jesus and by His shed blood, go!"

It fought back vigorously for half an hour. Thousands were watching this dramatic deliverance. It was a classic battle between good and evil, between light and darkness, between heaven and hell.

Finally, with a scream, the foul spirit left. We stood the girl up. She blinked, looked confused. I could tell she was wondering who I was. She didn't even remember coming to the crusade. We led her to Christ, into the baptism of the Spirit, and put her in a local church. Since that night, I have had no doubt how powerful the name of Jesus is, and how tormenting the blood of Jesus is to the demonic kingdom.

Since 1982, I've led over 1.5 million people in India to Christ. Hell can't stop the work of Christ.

> *For though we walk in the flesh, we do not war according to the flesh. For the weapons of our warfare are not carnal but mighty in God for pulling down strongholds, casting down arguments and every high thing that exalts itself against the knowledge of God, bringing every thought into captivity to the obedience of Christ. (2 Corinthians 10:3-5)*

It's a lot easier to win a war when you're aware of the enemy's tactics and plans. The Bible exposes Satan for who he is and what he's trying to do to the church. There are no excuses for ignorance as we push back the kingdom of darkness. It is up to us to fully take up the authority we possess as we wage this war, but authority starts with humility:

> *Therefore humble yourselves under the mighty hand of God, that He may exalt you in due time, casting all your care upon Him, for He cares for you. Be sober, be vigilant; because your adversary the devil walks about like a roaring lion, seeking whom he may devour. (1 Peter 5:6-8)*

Here are a few weapons to put in your arsenal as you wage your own personal war in life:

Always stay prepared for battle:

> *Or what king, going to make war against another king, does not sit down first and consider whether he is able with ten thousand to meet him who comes against him with twenty thousand? (Luke 14:31)*

OUR WEAPONS	SATAN'S SCHEMES (Wiles)
His Blood	Subtle Living Temptations
The Word (Sword of the Spirit)	Lies
Obedience	Lust
Humility	False religion
Serving/ Volunteering	Deception
Gentleness	Twisting scripture
The Name of Jesus	Craftiness
Prayer/Fasting	Suggestion
Forgiving	Pride
God's Armor	Error
Love	Greed
Worship	Judgment
Meekness	Self Righteousness
Your Testimony	Hatred

"
All men can see
the tactics whereby
I conquer, but what
none can see is
the strategy out
of which the
victory evolved."
– *Sun Tzu*

CHAPTER 10

He Promised!

For all the promises of God in Him are Yes, and in Him Amen, to the glory of God through us. (2 Corinthians 1:20)

...imitate those who through faith and patience inherit the promises. (Hebrews 6:12)

Grace and peace be multiplied to you in the knowledge of God and of Jesus our Lord, as His divine power has given to us all things that pertain to life and godliness, through the knowledge of Him who called us by glory and virtue, by which have been given to us exceedingly great and precious promises, that through these you may be partakers of the divine nature, having escaped the corruption that is in the world through lust. (2 Peter 1:2-4)

I wrote a book a while back called *Shaking Hands with God*. It's a teaching of covenant promises and why our faith should never waver based on our heavenly Father's promises. As we know, a promise is a vow or declaration that something will or will not be done. A promise leads to expectations.

For example, my granddaughter caught her dad, Adam (my son), in one of those moments all of us parents have had.

"Dad can my friends and I go to a concert?"

Adam said, "Sure, no problem."

"Promise Dad! You really promise?"

"Yes! I said yes, didn't I?"

When it was time to buy the three tickets he found out they were $150 a piece! Now what Dad? He bit the bullet and bought them.

A promise is a promise! If you break your word enough to a spouse or a child, eventually they won't believe one thing you say.

> *In hope of eternal life which God, who cannot lie, promised before time began. (Titus 1:2)*

It doesn't say He won't lie; it says He *cannot* lie!

I love the Old Testament. I've learned a lot about spiritual warfare by studying some of the conventional ways God's people, Israel, conquered the Promised Land.

The biggest little word in the Bible is the word *if*. Webster tells us *if* means *in the event that or on condition that.* Here's a good example of what I'm talking about:

> *Now it shall come to pass, if you diligently obey the voice of the Lord your God, to observe carefully all His*

commandments which I command you today, that the
Lord your God will set you high above nations of the earth.
(Deuteronomy 28:1)

God issues a promise but with a condition, "I will, if you will."

I like simple theology. God's promises are solid and just. He
will always deliver on His word, like my son Adam had to do.
We have to know that we serve an unchanging God. Who He
was yesterday, a deliverer, a healer, a provider, is who we will
find in Him today — in our daily lives and our future lives.

In Exodus, we read the story of Moses who led God's people
out of bondage and slavery in Egypt into the Promised Land.
The Children of Israel were at the end of their rope. In Chapter
Two we see the king of Egypt has died, and the children of
Israel are crying uncle to a God they have largely ignored.

Now it happened in the process of time that the king of
Egypt died. Then the children of Israel groaned because
of the bondage, and they cried out, and their cry came
up to God because of the bondage. So God heard their
groaning, and God remembered His covenant with
Abraham, with Isaac, and with Jacob. And God looked
upon the children of Israel, and God acknowledged them.
(Exodus 2:23-25)

God's covenant chosen people were living as slaves in Egypt.
Finally, because they were sick and tired of being sick and
tired, they called upon the living God. God heard them.

You have to know, God isn't motivated or moved out of

sentiment, but by promise (covenant). Four hundred years before this, Abraham, the Father of these children, knew God. God Himself made a promise to Abraham, who was then called Abram:

> Now the Lord had said to Abram: Get out of your country, from your family and from your father's house, To a land that I will show you. I will make you a great nation; I will bless you and make your name great, and you shall be a blessing. I will bless those who bless you, and I will curse him who curses you; and in you all the families of the earth shall be blessed. (Genesis 12:1-3)

God had great plans for the Children of Israel. He made a promise and kept it. They had to hold up their end of the deal too. We see in Exodus that He provided everything they needed for the journey into the land of promise: daily food that fell from the air, a cloud by day and a pillar of fire by night, water from a rock…

When God makes a promise, He's faithful in every way and in every detail to keep that promise.

It didn't take the Children of Israel long to get out of Egypt, but it took forty years to get Egypt out of them. Doubt, complaining, and generations of bondage weren't easy to shake off. In the end, we see God made good on His promise. He brought them to a land filled with milk and honey. The road may have been bumpy but with God a promise is a promise!

" Invincibility lies in the defense, the possibility of victory in the attack."

— *Sun Tzu*

" Victory at all cost,
victory in spite
of all terror,
victory however
long and hard
the road may be;
for without
victory, there is
no survival."
— *Winston Churchill*

CHAPTER 11

The Prophetic and Warfare

This charge I commit to you, son Timothy, according to the prophecies previously made concerning you, that by them you may wage the good warfare (1 Timothy 1:18)

Here Paul reminds young Timothy, who ran a little scared at times, to remember the prophecies spoken over him. Paul tells him they are part of his arsenal.

Over the last three, almost four decades, I've had several prophetic words spoken over me by gifted, anointed, well-known ministers, and even a couple of complete strangers.

In 1978, I was at a conference in Fresno, California. As I was looking at the speaker's product table, a gentleman approached me and asked if he could pray for me. At first, I was reluctant because I had already seen a lot of what I call *parking lot prophets* do some weird things for money or influence, but his gentle face and demeanor seemed safe.

"Sure, go ahead," I said.

He began crying and prophesying, "God, why do I see this man standing before thousands, no hundreds of thousands of dark-skinned people on the sand with palm trees all around and the glory all around him as he preaches?"

Now remember, I was barely saved. My hair still wet from the baptistery, so to speak. At that time, I was happy with my construction job, and content to be saved and in a good church. I wondered why this man would see or say all this? Four years later, in 1982, I was in India doing exactly what he saw.

In 1978, I was living in Paradise, California, a beautiful mountain town on the western slope of the Sierra Nevada Mountains. I never wanted to leave. It was a hunter and fisherman's paradise, and I had it all in my backyard.

But that year I had a dream: In the dream, I was back in my hometown, San Jose, preaching in a building with a tile roof, red carpet, and pews. My whole family was sitting in the front row listening intently to me. Me? Preaching? I woke up and told Carla my dream.

She said, "Well, Honey, maybe God is calling you to be a Pastor in San Jose."

I laughed out loud, and I thought to myself, "If God ever gets that desperate, His Kingdom is in real trouble."

In 1985, we moved into that very building, red carpet, tiled roof, pews... and, yes, my family was saved and sitting on the front row listening to me.

I'm a big believer in prophetic dreams and visions. Most of the words spoken over me have come to pass, but there are still a few I'm waiting to see happen in my lifetime. So, like Timothy, I'm waging a good warfare for them!

One of the biggest battles pastors and churches have is obtaining land — land that's ours with buildings we build for God's glory. In Silicon Valley land is uber expensive. We have to compete with companies such as Apple, Intel, Facebook, Google, and Cisco, to name a few. So, you can guess who gets the premium land. You've heard the old saying, "What's the golden rule? The one with the gold rules."

Even though we didn't have the financial backing that Apple, Facebook, and the others had, we were able to lease a computer warehouse that became our place of worship (the one with the red tiled roof). Just across the street, however, was open land. Next to the open land were two big, wonderful buildings.

In those days, we often would bring in prophets to minister and prophesy to our people. Three of them, unbeknownst to each other, all prophesied the very same thing to me, "I see three buildings in a row; all paid for!"

Needless to say, I set my sights on the land across the street. I didn't have any idea of the knowing battles we would face before we got that land! We had some serious warfare with our city, the Army Corps of Engineers, the Sierra club, and Friends of the Flowers. They all tried to stop us from building our church. It was war!

We fasted, we prayed, we went before the city council, we hired lawyers, we prophesied over the property, and ultimately we won!

Interesting sidebar: Back in the day, the family that owned the land we bought was the Lord family. Folks called that property the Lord's Land.

God gave Adam and Eve property called a garden in a place called Eden. Satan usurped Adam's authority and got Adam and Eve evicted. Since that time, God's people have been fighting to get land back. Have you ever noticed what God promised Abram about land?

Now the Lord had said to Abram:

> "Get out of your country, from your family and from your father's house, To a land that I will show you. I will make you a great nation; I will bless you and make your name great; and you shall be a blessing. I will bless those who bless you, and I will curse him who curses you; And in you all the families of the east shall be blessed." (Genesis 12:1-3)

"To a land I will show you?" What did Abram (Abraham) want more than anything else? A son! What did God want for him? Land, The Promised Land! God said, first occupy the Promised Land, and then you'll have way more than one son. Your descendants will be like stars of heaven and the grains of sand on the seashore. Isn't it interesting that the squabble in Israel over land is still ongoing?

The devil hates it when God's people own land. Whether it's land for our churches, for our houses, or for our businesses, he will fight fang and nail to stop us, using every trick in the book. Remember, we wrestle not against flesh and blood (people), but we do war against the powers of darkness.

Since Israel became a nation, in 1948, and began occupying their promised land, the end-time prophetic clock seemed to tick just a little faster.

CHAPTER 12

The Worshipping Warrior

When we welcome the Holy Spirit into God's house, we want, as on the day of Pentecost, the place to be filled and the people to be filled. Jesus didn't turn water into wine until the pots were filled. For our cup to run over, it must first be filled. Then the overflow will come.

One of the many weapons in our arsenal that we Christians have and should use daily is worship. How confusing it is to our enemy, that in the midst of war, we lift our hearts, our heads, and our hands to our God, knowing He will make a way. Our weapons are mighty indeed!

One thing I've always loved about our church is our praise and worship. We make sure every service starts with a corporate time of praising our risen Lord and worshipping our heavenly Father. I believe presence invites power. Spirit-filled people like a spirit-filled worship service where they can lift their hands, clap their hands, bow their knees, or even prostrate themselves before the Lord and worship Him with tears, shouts, and laughter. It all happens at Jubilee during praise and worship.

It's wonderful what God can do to one's heart during a worship service. Hard hearts become softened to the point they're ready to receive the seed of the Word. Hosea put it this way:

Ephraim is a trained heifer that loves to thresh grain; but I harnessed her fair neck, I will make Ephraim pull a plow. Judah shall plow; Jacob shall break his clods. Sow for yourselves righteousness; reap in mercy; break up your fallow ground, for it is time to seek the Lord, till He comes and rains righteousness on you. (Hosea 10:11-12)

Judah means praise. Praise plows the ground so the seed can be sown and watered by prayer. Then comes the harvest.

Many times I have ministered out of 2 Chronicles, where God told King Jehoshaphat to send the band and the singers to go before the soldiers and worship:

So they rose early in the morning and went out into the Wilderness of Tekoa; and as they went out, Jehoshaphat stood and said, "Hear me, O Judah and you inhabitants of Jerusalem: Believe in the Lord your God, and you shall be established; believe His prophets, and you shall prosper." And when he had consulted with the people, he appointed those who should sing to the Lord, and who should praise the beauty of holiness, as they went out before the army and were saying: "Praise the Lord, for His mercy endures forever. Now when they began to sing and to praise, the Lord set ambushes against the people of Ammon, Moab, and Mount Seir, who had come against Judah; and they were defeated. (2 Chronicles 20:20-22)

When they sang, God went to work! It must torment the devil to a near meltdown to know he's been replaced as the worship leader of the Host by us, the body of Christ.

Here's a scripture for New Testament believers:

Speaking to one another in psalms and hymns and spiritual songs, singing and making melody in your heart to the Lord, giving thanks always for all things to God the Father in the name of our Lord Jesus Christ (Ephesians 5:19-20)

Elijah heard a sound of abundance coming to God's people who had been backslidden for years.

Then Elijah said to Ahab, "Go up, eat and drink; for there is the sound of abundance of rain." (1 Kings 18:41)

I believe when we gather together as a church body and sing to the Lord, it opens the heavens above us and blessings flow down upon God's people. I've always enjoyed reading these passages from Isaiah:

"Sing, O barren, you who have not borne! Break forth into singing, and cry aloud, you who have not labored with child! For more are the children of the desolate than the children of the married woman," says the Lord. "Enlarge the place of your tent, and let them stretch out the curtains of your dwellings; do not spare; lengthen your cords, and strengthen your stakes. For you shall expand to the right and to the left, and your descendants will inherit the nations, And make the desolate cities inhabited. "Do not fear, for you will not be ashamed;

neither be disgraced, for you will not be put to shame;
for you will forget the shame of your youth, and will not
remember the reproach of your widowhood anymore.
For your maker is your husband, The Lord of hosts is
His name; and your Redeemer is the Holy One of Israel;
He is called the God of the whole earth." (Isaiah 54:1-5)

"For you shall go out with joy, and be led out with
peace; the mountains and the hills shall break forth
into singing before you, and all the trees of the field
shall clap their hands. Instead of the thorn shall come
up the cypress tree, And instead of the brier shall come
up the myrtle tree; And it shall be to the Lord for a
name, For an everlasting sign that shall not be cut off."
(Isaiah 55:12-13)

Sing o barren, sing it loud!

" Victory is won not in miles, but in inches. Win a little now, hold your ground, and later, win a little more."

— *Louis L'Amour*

CHAPTER 13

Giving That Leads to Breakthrough

One of the most powerful portions of scripture, to me, is found in the 22nd chapter of Genesis. It's a landmark story of absolute faith and trust under constant testing. Faith is a force! It grows like a muscle with exercise. I call faith the currency of heaven because it purchases, obtains promises, claims, releases, and so much more.

Father Abraham's faith was tested:

> *Now it came to pass after these things that God tested Abraham, and said to him, "Abraham!" And he said, "Here I am." Then He said, "Take now your son, your only son Isaac, whom you love, and go to the land of Moriah, and offer him there as a burnt offering on one of the mountains of which I shall tell you." (Genesis 22:1-2)*

Know the difference: Satan tempts, God tests. Strong faith comes from strong trials and hard times. I've discovered this to be true in my walk with God. How long did old Abraham wait for his precious son, Isaac? Decades!

Is this one of those stories of "The Lord giveth, and the Lord taketh away?" What is God looking for here? An offering. He asked Abraham to give Him a sacrifice of that which Abraham loved more than his own life — his son.

As we know, Abraham obeyed God. He went to Mount Moriah, ready to give to God the thing he treasured most — Isaac!

> *And Abraham stretched out his hand and took the knife to slay his son. But the Angel of the Lord called to him from heaven and said, "Abraham, Abraham!" So he said, "Here I am." And He said, "Do not lay your hand on the lad, or do anything to him; for now I know that you fear God, since you have not withheld your son, your only son, from Me." Then Abraham lifted his eyes and looked, and there behind him was a ram caught in a thicket by its horns. So Abraham went and took the ram, and offered it up for a burnt offering instead of his son. And Abraham called the name of the place, The-Lord-Will-Provide; as it is said to this day, "In the Mount of the Lord it shall be provided." (Genesis 22:10-14)*

God said, in verse 12, "Now I know…" Know what, exactly? "You did not withhold."

Man is the only creation of God that has the free will to withhold or hold back. The earth doesn't withhold its life; the clouds don't horde up the blessing of rain, and animals don't withhold multiplying and keeping their species from extinction. The apple tree doesn't withhold its beautiful fruit. Ah, but man! Man can withhold praise, time, honor, tithes, and offerings to God, and still go about breathing God's air, enjoying a sunset, gazing at the stars, getting up in the morning and never thinking about offering anything to God.

Every breakthrough I've had in my Christian life followed some special offering I gave to God — a sacrifice, giving something I owned!

I'm baffled by how few church-going Christians tithe. I think it's mostly out of fear. But there are some who think they have a higher revelation. They think tithing is passé. I've heard every lame argument against it since I began ministering. To this day, I have yet to see one of those people prosper who fought against the tithe. The ones I know ended up losing what they had.

As for me and my house, we tithe and we give offerings! It's a weapon of our warfare. It opens doors, even windows.

> *Will a man rob God? Yet you have robbed Me! But you say, 'In what way have we robbed You?' In tithes and offerings. You are cursed with a curse, for you have robbed Me, even this whole nation. Bring all the tithes into the storehouse, that there may be food in My house, and try Me now in this," Says the Lord of hosts, "If I will not open for you the windows of heaven and pour out for you such blessing that there will not be room enough to receive it. "And I will rebuke the devourer for your sakes, so that he will not destroy the fruit of your ground, nor shall the vine fail to bear fruit for you in the field," Says the Lord of hosts; "And all nations will call you blessed, for you will be a delightful land," Says the Lord of hosts" (Malachi 3:8-12)*

Once I first read that, I was all in!

For God so loved the world — one full of sinners, I might add — He gave...He gave his beloved son to us.

In 1984, Carla and I sold our house and gave the whole amount to our fledgling church, because the church desperately needed the money.

Just a few years later, a businessman in Silicon Valley bought us a house on a golf course. I have since sold it and gave the money to the church. I like to keep giving. It drives the devil nuts!

Don't hold back. Lucifer held back praise and honor to God and look what happened!

> *Give, and it will be given to you: good measure, pressed down, shaken together, and running over will be put into your bosom. For with the same measure that you use, it will be measured back to you. (Luke 6:38)*

> *But this I say: He who sows sparingly will also reap sparingly, and he who sows bountifully will also reap bountifully. So let each one give as he purposes in his heart, not grudgingly or of necessity; for God loves a cheerful giver. And God is able to make all grace abound toward you, that you, always having all sufficiency in all things, may have an abundance for every good work. As it is written: "He has dispersed abroad, He has given to the poor; His righteousness endures forever." Now may He who supplies seed to the sower, and bread for*

food, supply and multiply the seed you have sown and increase the fruits of your righteousness, while you are enriched in everything for all liberality, which causes thanksgiving through us to God. (2 Corinthians 9:6-11)

God doesn't need our money; He's God. He owns the cattle on a thousand hills. But you have to know, one of the most powerful weapons of our Christian warfare is the weapon of giving with a humble and grateful heart. Giving is actually a relational issue, not a burden. It shows our trust in Him. It's an act of worship!

" There is no victory at bargain basement prices."
— *Dwight D. Eisenhower*

" Many times we
miss out on God's
best because we
give up too soon.
We don't realize
how close we
are to victory."
— *Joel Osteen*

CHAPTER 14

Armor On!

Finally, my brethren, be strong in the Lord and in the power of His might. Put on the whole armor of God, that you may be able to stand against the wiles of the devil. For we do not wrestle against flesh and blood, but against principalities, against powers, against the rulers of the darkness of this age, against spiritual hosts of wickedness in the heavenly places. Therefore take up the whole armor of God, that you may be able to withstand in the evil day, and having done all, to stand. Stand therefore, having girded your waist with truth, having put on the breastplate of righteousness, and having shod your feet with the preparation of the gospel of peace; above all, taking the shield of faith with which you will be able to quench all the fiery darts of the wicked one. And take the helmet of salvation, and the sword of the Spirit, which is the word of God; praying always with all prayer and supplication in the Spirit, being watchful to this end with all perseverance and supplication for all the saints. (Ephesians 6:10-18)

"Finally," Paul writes to his beloved friends at Ephesus, "be strong in the Lord and in the power of this might!" Paul constantly reminded the early church that life, even with Christ, is a struggle.

Warfare! We have spiritual enemies to fight against, a Captain to fight for, a banner to fight under, and certain rules of war by which we are to govern. A smart soldier is first strong-hearted and then well-armed. He emphasizes "The whole armor of God." No one piece can be ignored. We, humans, have no defense against the powerful, unseen, or ancient powers, so we need the armor of God. It has God's signature on it! He designed it. It fits all of us perfectly. Paul stresses, "That you may be able to stand against the wiles (tricks) of the devil."

To stand against the devil is really to take a stand against sin; sin that constantly tempts us. God warned Cain:

> So the Lord said to Cain, "Why are you angry? And why has your countenance fallen? If you do well, will you not be accepted? And if you do not dso well, sin lies at the door. And its desire is for you, but you should rule over it." (Genesis 4:6-7)

God's armor for us is primarily defensive in nature. The constant onslaught from principalities, powers, rulers of darkness, and wicked unclean spirits begs us to stay fully covered, and have no exposed areas for fiery darts to penetrate, having done all, to stand. I would say all we know to do and can do, as we read in scriptures, is to pray and be submitted to God's house, and to stand strong.

As Paul begins to categorize the various pieces of armor, obviously getting revelation from observing a Roman Soldier fully dressed for battle, he starts with the belt.

It all starts with truth, the belt or girdle of truth! It doesn't begin with one's faith. If one's faith isn't based on and in truth, then one's religion is built on error or lies. Jesus said, "I am the way, the truth, and the life." The soldier's belt holds everything together as well as gives a place to sheath one's sword and dagger.

Next is the breastplate of righteousness. This protects our vitals, especially the heart and the lungs. Paul also refers to it as a breastplate of faith and love.

> But let us who are of the day be sober, putting on the breastplate of faith and love, and as a helmet the hope of salvation. (1 Thessalonians 5:8)

Our love has to be constantly protected, or we will slip into unforgiveness and bitterness.

Let's look at the soldier's feet. When I think of shodding or to shod, my mind goes back to when I was a kid. My dad had horses, and every so often they needed to be shod. The man who would come by would put metal horseshoes on the bottom of Dad's horses to protect their feet. The Greek called it hupodeo, which means protecting the feet. The Roman soldiers' feet, likewise, had to be protected. They also had spike-like attachments secured to the bottoms for footing, a bit like golfer's spikes, or football and baseball cleats, all to help the athlete get better footing. The Christian soldiers' feet take them to the world so they can proclaim the blessed gospel of peace to one and all.

Next, "...above all taking the shield of faith." Paul loved preaching and teaching on grace and faith. The Roman soldiers' chief defensive piece of equipment was his shield. It could withstand arrows, swords, blows, rocks or whatever the enemy came at him with. It was mobile. Satan's fiery darts are thoughts he tries to plant in our minds to discourage us, bring doubts, fears, and temptations. The Bible tells us we overcome the world by our faith.

The helmet of salvation! Of course, the helmet is vital. It protected the soldier's head and brain. Ever notice in football the last thing a player does before entering the game is put on his helmet. Same with baseball players, they wear a protective batter's cap before stepping up to the plate. Here in California, we have helmet laws for motorcycles to protect riders from injury or even death. The believers must be protected. Thoughts about our salvation come to one and all at times. The devil constantly brings into question the validity of God's Word and God's promises.

We give altar calls at Jubilee nearly every service. Often I see the same folks continually come up for prayer, the sinner's prayer. Finally, I asked one fella, "Why do you keep coming forward to get saved?"

He chuckled, "Pastor, I just like to be sure."

I said, "Man, keep that helmet on. Sleep with it on."

"I'll try, Pastor, I'll try," he replied.

> *Whoever confesses that Jesus is the Son of God, God abides in him, and he in God. (1 John 4:15)*

> *I beseech you therefore, brethren, by the mercies of God, that you present your bodies a living sacrifice, holy, acceptable to God, which is your reasonable service. And do not be conformed to this world, but be transformed by the renewing of your mind, that you may prove what is that good and acceptable and perfect will of God. (Romans 12:1-2)*

Let's protect God's word that rules our hearts and minds. Time to get on the offensive!

Take the sword of the spirit, which is the Word of God in your mouth. The Word, coming out of your mouth, is like swinging a razor-sharp, two-edged sword at the powers of darkness. Jesus did it in the wilderness with, "It is written." The devil has no defense against God's spoken Word:

> *For the word of God is living and powerful, and sharper than any two-edged sword, piercing even to the division of soul and spirit, and of joints and marrow, and is a discerner of the thoughts and intents of the heart. (Hebrews 4:12)*

> *Then I turned to see the voice that spoke with me. And having turned I saw seven golden lampstands, and in the midst of the seven lampstands One like the Son*

of Man, clothed with a garment down to the feet and girded about the chest with a golden band. His head and hair were white like wool, as white as snow, and His eyes like a flame of fire; His feet were like fine brass, as if refined in a furnace, and His voice as the sound of many waters; 16 He had in His right hand seven stars, out of His mouth went a sharp two-edged sword, and His countenance was like the sun shining in its strength (Revelation 1:12–16)

The lamb is now a Lion-King.

Paul reminds us:

...praying always with all prayer and supplication in the Spirit, being watchful to this end with all perseverance and supplication for all the saints. (Ephesians 6:18)

It all starts with prayer and ends with prayer. My prayer today for you is, "You are strong, victorious, overcoming, and the devil 's worst nightmare!"

Amen!

" In war there is no substitute for victory."
— *General Douglas MacArthur*

CHAPTER 15

God's Strategy – Satan's Strongholds!

Years ago, I did a survey of the various cities that make up the whole Bay Area. I did a weekly television program on a popular Christian network that went around most of the world.

We called the survey process mapping - spiritual mapping (discerning) — identifying the biggest obstacles to the Gospel in various cities all across America. I began with my own back yard, the San Francisco Bay Area, a world famous region for many reasons. The City by the Bay, as it is often referred to, is a world-class city for tourism and commerce. Silicon Valley, where I live, is just forty-five miles or so south of The City. Four miles from downtown San Francisco, due east is Oakland. These are each drastically unique cities, yet just a rock's throw away from each other.

Some cities we surveyed had a gospel footprint while others, like San Francisco, not so much. I began looking at origins of cities: Who came, who built them and why? What kinds of people were attracted to certain areas, and neighborhoods?

Why was there so much crime in some cities while not others? Why did the gay community, hippie, and bohemian types flock to San Francisco? What attracted Apple, Intel, Facebook, and Google to Silicon Valley?

I gathered information from libraries, police departments, schools, museums, and the like. Once I had a grasp of where resistance came from and why it was directed toward the Gospel, church, the Bible, and the Christian world-view, I then could plan a prayer strategy. Our next step was to gather an army of prayer warriors and surround one of the cities. We even chartered a boat so that we could go around the entire Bay Area. We drove over the Golden Gate and Bay Bridges. We went to mountaintops and building tops and interceded for our beloved Bay Area. We brought in well-known ministers to hold rallies downtown.

Oh, the devil pushed back hard. It was war! It's still raging to this day, but we haven't lost heart even though at times it seems like we will never see revival in the Bay Area, but the answer is, "Yes! We will see revival!"

STRONGHOLDS

A dear friend, and neighbor, Dr. Ed Silvoso, founder and president of Harvest Evangelism, is very knowledgeable in the area of demonic strongholds. In his booklet, *Strongholds, What They Are and How to Pull Them Down*, he writes: "Spiritual strongholds are satan's secret weapon in waging battle. It is through the surreptitious use of strongholds that satan controls the behavior of believers and as a result, the behavior of the church. These strongholds must be identified and destroyed for the Christian to become victorious and for the church to regain control of the heavenlies." Ed's definition of a stronghold is this: "A spiritual stronghold is a mind-set impregnated with hopelessness that causes us to accept as unchangeable, situations that we know are contrary to the will of God."

GOD'S STRATEGY

Regardless of where you live, know your God, know your calling, know your city, know your enemy, and never, ever stop praying!

> For the weapons of our warfare are not carnal but mighty in God for pulling down strongholds. (2 Corinthians 10:4)

We are commissioned, anointed if you will, to pull down strongholds. What exactly are we to pull down? In 2 Corinthians 10:5, we see, "...casting down arguments and every high thing that exalts itself against the knowledge of God, bringing every thought into captivity to the obedience of Christ."

Interestingly, we see this Scripture specifically talk about our thoughts. In my many years of pastoring and counseling, I can say most of the struggles that we believers deal with begin with a thought.

We know God's thoughts and ways are higher than ours. When our thoughts don't align with God's Word and promises, we have problems because our minds are open to hearing and entertaining arguments from the enemy against the truth of God's Word. Often strongholds originate in our thought processes. Fears and lies we believe originated first as thoughts that we agreed with the enemy, giving him the right to then torment us.

In the Old Testament, in particular, a stronghold was a fortified place. Let's examine this scripture:

> *And David stayed in strongholds in the wilderness and remained in the mountains in the Wilderness of Ziph. Saul sought him every day, but God did not deliver him into his hand. So David saw that Saul had come out to seek his life. And David was in the Wilderness of Ziph in a forest. (1 Samuel 23:14-15)*

David was running from King Saul. Here, David's hiding place was referred to as a stronghold. Caves and mountaintops made great strongholds because they were hard for an enemy to charge upon or mount an attack against. Spiritually speaking, a stronghold is a fixed mindset that causes a person to think or say to himself (or herself), "This is what I am, what I believe, and you won't change me." A stronghold can also come through generational curses like racism, gender hatred, addiction, even a religion or national culture. These strongholds all build defenses against God and the light and truth of His Word. Satan, Paul says, has blinded the masses:

> *But even if our gospel is veiled, it is veiled to those who are perishing, whose minds the god of this age has blinded, who do not believe, lest the light of the gospel of the glory of Christ, who is the image of God, should shine on them. (2 Corinthians 4:3-4)*

With so much resistance against the Christian faith, what do we do? I often refer to the law of opposites. The world and Satan have time-proven weapons: hate, violence, revenge, lies, greed, lust, political powers, fame, pride and so on. As Christians, we are in the world, but not of it! We are humans, but not mere humans.

Paul said, "We have God in us, and His Spirit to guide us." We have the mind of Christ, so we fight:

- Hate *with* Love & Forgiveness
- Violence *with* Meekness & Giving it to God
- Lies *with* Telling the Truth
- Political Powers *with* Prayers for All in Authority
- Fame *with* My Identity in Christ
- Greed *with* Generosity
- Pride *with* Humility

What do we do with atheists, church haters, far left-leaning liberals, people who believe in gay rights, and others who don't even come close to seeing eye-to-eye with our Christian view of life and eternity?

Love them. Just love them anyway!

Recently, an avowed, proud atheist reluctantly visited our church, because a friend brought him. Although he kept telling her that his mind was made up that he wasn't going to like it, shockingly, he did! He liked everything from the worship, the young people ('cool' people as he said) doing announcements, the charities, and me doing my thing. Today, he is a member — saved, filled and on fire. When asked why, he said it was the love he felt from those he encountered that very first day that hooked him.

Here's another story: A couple of years back a well-dressed middle-aged woman caught me after service and asked if I would pray for her.

"Sure," I said, "What's going on in your life?"

She began to cry, "Pastor, my lover left me, and I desperately want her back."

I said, "Oh, okay let's see, let's pray like Jesus taught us to pray,"

> *Seek first the kingdom of God and His righteousness, and all these things shall be added to you. Therefore do not worry about tomorrow, for tomorrow will worry about its own things. Sufficient for the day is its own trouble. (Matthew 6:33-34)*

After we prayed, she said, "Pastor you know why I come to Jubilee?"

"No," I answered.

"Pastor, I know you don't agree with my lifestyle, but I know you love me."

I said, "Yes, my sister, I do."

Love covers. It doesn't judge or expose. It's the love of God leads us to repentance.

CHAPTER 16

Warfare in the Church

Then they went into Capernaum, and immediately on the Sabbath He entered the synagogue and taught. And they were astonished at His teaching, for He taught them as one having authority, and not as the scribes. Now there was a man in their synagogue with an unclean spirit. And he cried out, saying, "Let us alone! What have we to do with You, Jesus of Nazareth? Did You come to destroy us? I know who You are — the Holy One of God!" But Jesus rebuked him, saying, "Be quiet, and come out of him!" And when the unclean spirit had convulsed him and cried out with a loud voice, he came out of him. Then they were all amazed, so that they questioned among themselves, saying, "What is this? What new doctrine is this? For with authority He commands even the unclean spirits, and they obey Him." (Mark 1:21-27)

Here in the Gospel of Mark, we see the first demon Jesus confronts and casts out is in a church, the synagogue at Capernaum.

Years ago I wrote a book, *When Lucifer and Jezebel Join Your Church*. The book was about my personal experience of people coming to Jubilee: people with unclean spirits, wolves in sheep's clothing, evil men preying on young boys for sexual favors, greedy sharks with crazy investment schemes looking to put the bite on gullible church members, false parking lot prophets trying to manipulate people through false prophecies. One guy joined the choir just to prey on one of our young sisters.

Tares amongst the wheat as Jesus called them. Here in our text, the Lord only knows how long this demon had been coming to the synagogue hiding inside the poor Jewish man.

There is a spirit we call a religious spirit. People with a religious spirit are always seeking a platform. At first, they may seem like a gift from God. They get close to leadership. They volunteer for everything. They open their homes for small groups. They come to every service, sitting as close to the front of the church as possible to be seen. Often they are overly friendly, even bringing gifts for the Pastor or his wife.

It all seems innocent and good until the mask comes off and the serpent raises his head like a cobra.

The first ten years of our church, from 1980-1990, we had it all. Because we were a new, fast growing work, church hoppers came, looking for the next new and exciting thing.

Of course, we were blessed with many wonderful folks, some who are still with us today. However, with eagles also come turkeys. Some of my biggest battles, sleepless nights, and heartaches came from wanting so badly to not believe that brother so-and-so or sister such-and-such was evil or of another spirit. We, Pastors, love people. We want to help everyone. It's hard to believe people would use the house of God for their personal desires, yet, it's been going on for more than 2,000 years. There's nothing new under the sun:

As you therefore have received Christ Jesus the Lord, so walk in Him, rooted and built up in Him and established in the faith, as you have been taught, abounding in it with thanksgiving. Beware lest anyone cheat you through philosophy and empty deceit, according to the tradition of men, according to the basic principles of the world, and not according to Christ. (Colossians 2:6-8)

Religious spirits that fought him over sound doctrine constantly challenged Paul:

Finally, my brethren, rejoice in the Lord. For me to write the same things to you is not tedious, but for you it is safe. Beware of dogs, beware of evil workers, beware of the mutilation! For we are the circumcision, who worship God in the Spirit, rejoice in Christ Jesus, and have no confidence in the flesh. (Philippians 3:1-3)

Jesus warned his disciples to beware of the leaven of the Pharisees. Over the last three decades, I have counseled with and heard horror stories of Pastors putting some young upstart in a position of power and all hell breaking loose. It is known as the Absalom spirit surfacing, a real spirit that is set on destroying churches. If the associate thinks he's smarter, more anointed than the Senior Pastor, he begins to spread leaven amongst the members. If he can't get more power he leaves, tries to split the church, and tries to start his own church down the street.

I have yet to see one of these works succeed. God doesn't like rebellion and self-righteousness. I let a singles adult leader share one Sunday while I was touring Israel with church members. He announced he was starting his own church the following week. I couldn't believe it when I returned. I had just given the man a car as a gift. Whatever happened to him and his so called church? Yeah, you guessed it — it never grew, and I haven't heard a word about him for years.

One pastor friend from up in Oregon got sick and needed a leave of absence. While the pastor was on sabbatical, the assistant talked the board into firing my friend and putting him in as the new senior pastor. This almost killed my friend. He never really recovered. He turned to alcohol and nearly died from liver disease. He moved to San Jose and joined our church. I would see him from the pulpit forlorn, dark, and sad, and it hurt me. I wanted so bad to preach him happy or help him get with it or get over it, but I couldn't.

Eventually, he disappeared with his poor little wife and kids, and I lost track of him. I still think about him now and then and wonder just how successful his old church is with Lucifer in the pulpit. Self-righteousness and pride are always looking for a host to damage the kingdom of God.

I told one Pastor who suffered an ugly church split, Brother, don't feel that bad. God had the original church split when

His assistant Lucifer took one-third of the angels and left." He laughed, but he was still hurting.

Don't ever follow someone who has a divisive spirit, one who gossips, slanders, speaks evil of God's servants. A so-called prophet attended our church years ago. He began looking for sharp young men. He started his own Bible study with what he called higher revelation. It all fell apart after a while, and the young gullible followers are all backslid to this day.

If you're in a church, don't attend some small group that is not sanctioned by leadership because it's probably led by a lone wolf who is looking for his own sheep. Remember wolves are carnivorous. They love sheep meat. Pastors only ask for the wool, not the flesh:

> *Therefore take heed to yourselves and to all the flock, among which the Holy Spirit has made you overseers, to shepherd the church of God which He purchased with His own blood. For I know this, that after my departure savage wolves will come in among you, not sparing the flock. Also from among yourselves men will rise up, speaking perverse things, to draw away the disciples after themselves. (Act 20:28-30)*

" If you know the
enemy and you
know yourself,
your victory
will not stand in
doubt; if you know
heaven and you
know earth, you
may make your
victory complete."
— *Sun Tzu*

CHAPTER 17

Breaking Curses

For as many as are of the works of the law are under the curse; for it is written, "Cursed is everyone who does not continue in all things which are written in the book of the law, to do them." But that no one is justified by the law in the sight of God is evident, for "the just shall live by faith." Yet the law is not of faith, but "the man who does them shall live by them." Christ has redeemed us from the curse of the law, having become a curse for us (for it is written, "Cursed is everyone who hangs on a tree"), that the blessing of Abraham might come upon the Gentiles in Christ Jesus, that we might receive the promise of the Spirit through faith. (Galatians 3:10-14)

CAUSES OF, OR DOORS FOR CURSES

The average American Christian has little understanding of the power of curses, yet most believers on the mission field are well aware of their evil potential. We will examine cursed races, nations, cities, families and individuals.

Before moving on, let's define exactly what a curse is:

CURSE, n. A prayer for harm to befall someone or something; The harm resulting from an invocation; A profane oath; or something bringing or causing harm; scourge.

CURSE, v. To call down evil; to swear (Websters II-New Riverside Desk Dictionary)

In the Old Testament, the Hebrew word most commonly used for this concept, translated *curse* in English, is the word *arar*. Simply defined, the root word means, *to execrate, to abhor or detest someone or something.* This word is found in the passages in Deuteronomy, chapters 27 & 28, that deal with blessings and curses; "Cursed be he that..."

Several other Hebrew words are used to describe curses and cursing. These carry such meaning as *to bind under with an oath, to pierce, to vilify, to stab with words or to blaspheme.*

In the New Testament, the Greek words and their meanings are very similar to those in the Old Testament. Essentially, a curse removes the blessing of God and all that goes with it. Life itself is an expression of choice between the blessed life or being cursed.

Deuteronomy speaks of the blessings of obedience to God's laws and the curses of rebellion against them:

"I call heaven and earth as witnesses today against you, that I have set before you life and death, blessing and cursing; therefore choose life, that both you and your descendants may live." (Deuteronomy 30:19)

The key to the whole thing seems to revolve around two words: obedience and rebellion. The clearest example of this dichotomy is found in the creation story. God had blessed man and woman:

So God created man in His own image; in the image of God her created him; male and female He created them. Then God blessed them, and God said to them, "Be fruitful and multiply; fill the earth and subdue it, have dominion over the fish of the sea, over the birds of the air, and over every living thing that moves on the earth." (Genesis 1:27-28)

Along with the blessing came responsibility:

Then the Lord God took the man and put him in the garden of Eden to tend and keep it. And the Lord God commanded the man, saying, 'Of every tree of of the garden you may freely eat, but of the tree of the knowledge of good and evil you shall not eat, for in the day that you eat of it you shall surely die. (Genesis 2:15-17)

But Adam and Eve rebelled against God's command and curses followed. It is important to note that God didn't curse Adam and Eve whom He had blessed earlier. God cursed the ground because of their rebellion:

Then to Adam he said, 'Because you have heeded the voice of your wife, and have eaten from the tree of which I commanded you, saying, You shall not eat of it: Cursed is the ground for your sake; in toil you shall eat of it all the days of your life. Both thorns and thistles it shall bring forth for you, and you shall the herb of the field. In the sweat of your face you shall eat bread till you return to the ground, for out of it you were taken; for dust you are, and to dust shall return. (Genesis 3:17-19)

Did you notice that along with God's command to Adam and Eve came a warning?

But of the tree of the knowledge of good and evil you shall not eat, for in day that you eat of it you shall surely die. (Genesis 2:17)

As teachers and ministers of the gospel, *the Good News,* we tend to emphasize the blessings of following Jesus but neglect to warn people about the consequences of disobedience. Satan rebelled and got kicked out of Heaven. Adam rebelled and got kicked out of the Garden. Humanity rebels and gets kicked out of blessings.

Paul seemed to take the ministry of warning quite seriously. (See, Acts 20:31, Colossians 1:28 and 1 Thessalonians 5:14). That's why every year in our church I teach on both blessings and the responsibilities of being a follower of our Lord. We're told to count the cost, as well as to count our blessings.

Webster defines rebellion as open opposition to any authority. Let's return to Genesis for a sobering look at another form of rebellion:

And Noah began to be a farmer, and he planted a vineyard. Then he drank of the wine and was drunk, and became uncovered in his tent. And Ham, the father of Canaan, saw the nakedness of this father, and told his two brothers outside. But Shem and Japheth took a garment took a garment and laid it on both their shoulders, and went backwards and covered the nakedness of their father. Their faces were turned away, and they did not see their Father's nakedness. So Noah awoke from his wind and knew what his younger son had done to him. Then he said, "Cursed be Canaan; a servant of servants he shall be to his brethren." And he said, "Blessed be the Lord, the God of Shem, and may Canaan be his servant. May God enlarge Japheth, and may he dwell in the tents of Shem; and may Canaan be his servant." (Genesis 9:20-27)

A sad commentary on this tragic passage is that God had first pronounced a blessing on all of them:

So God blessed Noah and his sons, and said to them: "Be fruitful and multiply, and fill the earth." (Genesis 9:1)

What brought the curse on Canaan? This curse, by the way, is still operating today in one form or another. First of all, Noah got drunk. Here is a clear act of rebellion; the Bible says drunkenness is a sin. Having a vineyard or partaking of the fruit of the vine in moderation was acceptable, but getting plowed meant Noah had gone too far. Then, while old Noah was passed out, in walked his son Ham and, apparently, Ham's son, Canaan. They saw the nakedness of Noah and couldn't wait to blab it to Shem and Japheth [Some commentators submit that there might even have been some act of perversion between Ham or Canaan and sleeping, Noah]. Nevertheless, my point is this: Even though you may be an eyewitness to another's weakness with cold, hard, documented facts, the trumpeting of another's sin is blatantly inviting a curse upon yourself.

Shem and Japheth covered their Father's nakedness without even looking. Here is a lesson for today: If we look hard and long enough we will find fault, so why go looking? No Christ-like believer can truly enjoy the fall of a brother or sister. On the contrary, there is a blessing in covering another's shortcomings:

> Hatred stirs up strife, but love covers all sins. (Proverbs 10:12)

> Blessed is he whose trangression is forgiven, whose sin is covered. (Psalm 32:1)

The first atonement, or covering, was performed by God Himself:

> Also for Adam and his wife the Lord God made tunics of skin and clothed them. (Genesis 3:21)

Here we see sinful Adam and Eve being covered by a blood sacrifice and guilty humans clothed by the skin of innocent animals. Some suggest that this animal was a lamb, foreshadowing a later, greater atonement by the One who would lift the curse of the law.

If a blessing were a gift, a curse would be a debt. Both blessings and curses are characterized by a particular kind of nature and operation — a truth Moses expected to be understood by God's people. The Lord had some careful instruction for

His people before they crossed over into the Promised Land:

Behold, I set before you today a blessing and a curse: the blessing, if you obey the commandments of the Lord your God which I command you today; and the curse, if you do not obey the commandments of the Lord your God, but turn aside from the way which I command you today, to go after other gods which you have not known. Now it shall be, when the Lord your God has brought you into the land which you go to possess, that you shall put the blessing on Mount Gerizim and the curse on Mount Ebal. Are they not on the other side of the Jordan, toward the setting sun, in the land of the Canaanites who dwell in the plain opposite Gilgal, beside the terebinth trees of Moreh? For you will cross over the Jordan and go in to possess the land which the Lord your God is giving you, and you will possess it and dwell in it. And you shall be careful to observe all the statutes and judgments which I set before you today. (Deuteronomy 11:26-32)

Blessings and curses operate by predetermined laws in the same way that God established the natural laws of creation. Most of us wouldn't dare test God's law of gravity by jumping off a high-rise building. Many people think that because they are somehow a special case, God will intervene and alter the predetermined nature and operation of blessings and curses just for them.

A young couple living together out of wedlock came to me to find out why they weren't blessed. They were praying, giving and attending church, yet they were not experiencing the blessing of God. When I asked them why they weren't married they just looked at each other and shrugged their shoulders, "Pastor, we have two children and we've been together for several years."

"You need to get married now," I firmly replied. These new converts simply had no awareness of the laws that govern blessings and curses. Once enlightened, they agreed to hold the ceremony.

Many young couples or individuals come to me for financial counseling. Before meeting with them, I pull their giving record. If they come to me with a sad story of lack and are not tithers, I bring them to Malachi, chapter 3:

> *For I am the Lord, I do not change; Therefore you are not consumed, O sons of Jacob. Yet from the days of your fathers You have gone away from My ordinances And have not kept them. Return to Me, and I will return to you," Says the Lord of hosts. "But you said, 'In what way shall we return?' Will a man rob God? Yet you have robbed Me! But you say, 'In what way have we robbed You?' In tithes and offerings. You are cursed with a curse, For you have robbed Me, Even this whole nation. Bring all the tithes into the storehouse, That there may be food in My house, And try Me now in this," Says the Lord of hosts, "If I will not open for you the windows of heaven And pour out for you such blessing That there will not be room enough to receive it." (Malachi 3:6-10)*

These young folks genuinely love the Lord but don't realize their affection isn't enough to draw the blessings. A relationship with God, like any relationship, involves standards. We must recognize God's laws, acknowledge them, and embrace their truth because they reveal His character and will.

A sinner or a saint who is in conflict with these laws will reap the effects in the spirit, soul, body, and estate. The maladies of Deuteronomy, chapter 28, cover all these areas:

> *But it shall come to pass, if you do not obey the voice of the Lord your God, to observe carefully all His commandments and His statutes which I command you today, that all these curses will come upon you and overtake you: Cursed shall you be in the city, and cursed shall you be in the country. Cursed shall be your basket and your kneading bowl. Cursed shall be the fruit of your body and the produce of your land, the increase of your cattle and the offspring of your flocks. Cursed shall you be when you come in, and cursed shall you be when you go out. The Lord will send on you cursing, confusion, and rebuke in all that you set your hand to do, until you are destroyed and until you perish quickly, because of the wickedness of your doings in which you have forsaken Me. (Deuteronomy 28:15-20)*

> *The Lord will strike you with consumption, with fever, with inflammation, with severe burning fever, with the sword, with scorching, and with mildew; they shall pursue you until you perish. (Deuteronomy 28:22)*

The Lord will strike you with madness and blindness and confusion of heart. And you shall grope at noonday, as a blind man gropes in darkness; you shall not prosper in your ways; you shall be only oppressed and plundered continually, and no one shall save you. (Deuteronomy 28:28-29)

Your sons and your daughters shall be given to another people, and your eyes shall look and fail with longing for them all day long; and there shall be no strength in your hand. (Deuteronomy 28:32)

The Lord will bring you and the king whom you set over you to a nation which neither you nor your fathers have known, and there you shall serve other gods — wood and stone. The Lord will bring you and the king whom you set over you to a nation which neither you nor your fathers have known, and there you shall serve other gods—wood and stone. (Deuteronomy 28:36)

Moreover all these curses shall come upon you and pursue and overtake you, until you are destroyed, because you did not obey the voice of the Lord your God, to keep His commandments and His statutes which He commanded you. (Deuteronomy 28:45)

" If you walk in
God's divine
wisdom, you will
surely begin to see
a greater measure
of victory and
good success in
your life."
— *Joseph Prince*

" The first step
on the way
to victory is
to recognize
the enemy."
— *Corrie Ten Boom*

CHAPTER 18

Curses – Part 2

What are some of the symptoms one might suffer under a curse? Deuteronomy, chapter 28, gave us some examples, and I have listed others below. Let me add a word of caution here. Just because you or someone you know is afflicted in one or more of the ways mentioned, that doesn't prove the existence of the curse. But don't discount it either.

Here is a partial list of common symptoms of curses:

- Disturbed sleep
- Memory lapses
- Nightmares
- Confusion
- Headaches
- Hampered breathing
- Depression
- Heart palpitation/anxiety
- Generational alcoholism
- Continued financial woes
- Unexplained fatigue
- A rash of accidents
- Outbursts of anger
- Suicidal thoughts
- Premature death (especially running in one sex of the family)

Pastors, missionaries, and evangelists need to be on constant guard against such afflictions. Witches, covens, and the like are cursing many ministers on a daily basis, especially those in highly visible positions. How many times have ministers found themselves embroiled in marital spats, conflicts with rebellious children, staff mutinies, or financial problems that appear almost overnight? Often these situations are beyond natural explanations.

How can we protect ourselves against such curses, and what can we do about it if we find ourselves cursed? The most important first step in breaking a curse is to repent for allowing it to come:

> *Like a flitting sparrow, like a flying swallow, so a curse without cause shall not alight. (Proverbs 26:2)*

If you are suffering under the torment of a curse, somehow it found an opening. Do not get caught up with defending yourself; just repent. Also, make sure you relinquish any bitterness or unforgiveness in your heart. Take your rightful authority over the curse in the name of Jesus and rebuke it. Indeed, I apply the blood of Christ and invoke the name of Jesus when loosing someone or something from a curse.

Many people need understanding on what activities invite a curse, which in turn provides a platform for evil spirits:

> *And the person who turns to mediums and familiar spirits, to prostitute himself with them, I will set My face against that person and cut him off from his people. (Leviticus 20:6)*

> *Also he made his son pass through the fire, practiced soothsaying, used witchcraft, and consulted spiritists and mediums. He did much evil in the sight of the Lord, to provoke Him to anger. (II Kings 21:6)*

If you have ever been involved with fortunetellers, spiritualists, palm readers, tarot cards, Ouija boards, cults, hypnosis, witchcraft, séances, astrology or the like, put this book down right now and repent and renounce your involvement. Ask God for mercy, and break free from any hold these may have on you:

> *As he loved cursing, so let it come to him; As he did not delight in blessing, so let it be far from him. As he clothed himself with cursing as with his garment, So let it enter his body like water, And like oil into his bones. 19 Let it be to him like the garment which covers him, And for a belt with which he girds himself continually. Let this be the Lord's reward to my accusers, And to those who speak evil against my person. (Psalm 109:17-20)*

Pagans, witches and those who work their craft often hesitate to curse a believer. They know quite well that the curse, like a programmed missile, will find a target, but if the Christian resists in faith, the curse will come back to them. To ensure that this doesn't happen they tend to target those who are weak in the faith; the believer who isn't an obeyer, and the hearer who balks at being a doer. Among the easiest victims are those who discredit the power of the Holy Spirit and rely on mental assent for their protective armor. This victim will more than likely deny the very existence of curses, spells, hexes and the like. The powers of darkness thrive in ignorance:

My People are destroyed for lack of knowledge. Because you have rejected knowledge. (Hosea 4:6)

Ignorance is not the only point of vulnerability. What did Satan find in Peter and the other disciples that allowed him to secure permission to sift them like wheat?

Now there was also a dispute among them, as to which of them should be considered the greatest. And He said to them, "The kings of the Gentiles exercise lordship over them, and those who exercise authority over them are called 'benefactors.' But not so among you; on the contrary, he who is greatest among you, let him be as the younger, and he who governs as he who serves. For who is greater, he who sits at the table, or he who serves? Is it not he who sits at the table? Yet I am among you as the One who serves. "But you are those who have continued with Me in My trials. And I bestow upon you a kingdom, just as My Father bestowed one upon Me, that you may eat and drink at My table in My kingdom, and sit on thrones judging the twelve tribes of Israel." And the Lord said, "Simon, Simon! Indeed, Satan has asked for you, that he may sift you as wheat. But I have prayed for you, that your faith should not fail; and when you have returned to Me, strengthen your brethren." (Luke 22:24-32)

It very well could have been pride, as we look back to verse twenty-four:

There was also rivalry among them, as to which of them should be considered the greatest. (Luke 22:24)

Jesus constantly reminds His followers:

Therefore take heed that the light which is in you is not darkness. (Luke 11:35)

In my ministry, I have seen many other examples of potential demonic influence resulting from trauma. Two evil spirits will immediately enter a child who has been molested. Their names are Rejection and Rebellion. If these children are not delivered in Jesus' name, they will grow up emotionally warped. I have yet to deal with a homosexual seeking freedom who hasn't been abused in one way or another. Our prisons are full of rebellious and rejected people.

On New Year's Day, 1990, the first day of the uniquely important decade closing out the millennium, Carla and I, along with Ron Kenoly and thirty other believers, were in Tiananmen Square, in Beijing, China. Six months earlier the now-infamous massacre had taken place. We have learned that violence and murder serve as magnets for demonic strongholds. That day we were on a mission from God. With anointing oil (Isaiah 10:27), worship, prayer, and decrees, we broke the stronghold in the Spirit over Tiananmen Square. While armed guards looked on nearby, we blessed China and cursed communism. Within a few days, martial law was lifted, and the citizens of Beijing were allowed back on the Square.

One way a curse may take hold is when a marriage, friendship or some partnership goes sour. Love, loyalty, and commitment are good, but if these wonderful qualities become more fixed on human beings than on God, the results can be calamitous.

The term soul tie can be understood by such words as, *bonds, cleaving, or knitting.* Let me emphasize that there is also a positive side to this:

> *Therefore shall a man leave his father and his mother, and shall cleave unto his wife: and they shall be one flesh. (Genesis 2:24)*

One of my favorite stories in the Old Testament is found in 1 Samuel. It illustrates a positive soul-bond:

> *And it was so, when he had finished speaking to Saul, that the soul of Jonathan was knit to the soul of David. Jonathan loved him as his own soul. (1 Samuel 18:1)*

Here we see a deep friendship forming between two young men. The Bible also shows strong relational bonds between Abraham and Isaac, between David and his men, and between Paul and Timothy. Today, evangelists may be knit together with their prayer and financial partners, or pastors can have strong bonds with their flocks. Nothing is wrong with this until people begin to give more of their soul to each other than to God. Soul ties that begin positively, but turn negative are one way this kind of curse can take root.

The bonding of one's soul to another can also take place during acts of immorality:

> *...from the nations of who the Lord had said to the children of Israel, 'You shall not intermarry with them, nor they with you. For surely they will turn away your hearts after their Gods. (1 King 11:2)*

Soul ties can even take place between a person and an ideology. Demon-inspired writings can capture one's will and enslave it to false doctrines.

A minister friend of mine, widely well-known, had submitted himself and his ministry to another pastor. The pastor began to manipulate my friend, telling him things that simply weren't true, turning him from his friends and generally controlling his thoughts. My friend loved this pastor and believed everything he said. His ministry began to suffer. Others saw the problem, but couldn't convince him. Indeed, those in the grip of soul ties can be blind to reality.

Finally, the power of prayer prevailed, and my friend woke up as if from a dream. "This man has stolen my soul!" he roared over the phone to me. "I couldn't even hear from God without his help." As a result, he broke his unholy soul tie by repenting to God and forgiving the man and himself.

I have seen many people walk through life with part of their soul captured by another. One gentleman I know would tremble whenever a former colleague's name was mentioned. A lot of hurt and bitterness needed to be released before that soul link was finally broken.

This same pattern plagues many divorce cases. Sometimes even hatred is carried into another relationship, putting it in danger of falling prey to the same problems if the old ties aren't properly severed!

I once heard a pastor say, "Women seem to fall prey to curses more than men." As a pastor myself, I have to agree with that statement. It could have to do with the Bible's description of women as the weaker vessels (1 Peter 3:7), or perhaps is a result of Satan's special hatred for women that dates back to Genesis:

> *And I will put enmity between you and the woman, and between your seed and her Seed; he shall bruise your head, and you shall bruise His heel. (Genesis 3:15)*

Some women seem to be either exceptionally strong in the Lord or rather vulnerable. Satan was able to get to Adam through Eve. Satan today snares many men through women. The problem usually stems from man's unwillingness to lead, so the woman, out of frustration, will step up into the high-priestly role.

Here's an example: A couple in my office were in conflict because of rumors filtering through the church. When I addressed the husband the wife kept butting in answering for him. She was obviously angry and convinced the rumors were true. I tried my best to talk calmly to her husband, but he just sat there while she answered for him. Finally, I couldn't take it anymore and said, "Dear, please be quiet. I want to hear from your husband." She continued to ignore my request, so we were forced to end the conversation.

Friends, this is not an isolated problem. Because of a woman's vulnerability, a wife seeking to break a curse off herself or family should come under her husband's covering and protection:

> But I want you to know that the head of every man is Christ, the head of woman is man, and the head of Christ is God. (1 Corinthian 11:3)

Spiritually dysfunctional families are open targets for curses. Mothers playing the role of the father have unfortunately produced a generation of weak, confused, neurotic and, in some cases, homosexual men. It is worth noting the final words of the Old Testament:

> And he will turn the hearts of the father to the children, and the hearts of the children to their fathers, lest I come and strike the earth with a curse. (Malachi 4:6)

The God-given role of woman, wife, and mother is one of great honor and reward. The misguided women's rights movement is probably doing more to curse their own than anything else.

" I like to talk to
myself ahead
of time so when
temptation
comes, I've
already made
up my mind
that I have
the victory."
— *Joyce Meyer*

CHAPTER 19

Curses – Part 3

Not long ago I was ministering on the Hawaiian island of Maui, which the locals refer to as the island of the gods. My host spent years breaking powers of darkness over Maui, and the fruit of his labors can be seen in his ministry today. His church, a strong, growing fellowship in a land known for spewing out preachers, includes many locals who have to deal with the effects of generational bondages.

One day he was invited to a family's home to pray for a baby girl who was dying of a mysterious disorder. This family had been plagued with premature deaths among its females; even the female animals died.

As he entered the room where the dying infant lay, he felt a cold presence. His attention was drawn towards an old woman sitting in the corner. The grandmother looked like death incarnate. Right away, this astute minister knew that this affliction was the work of a curse. He prayed a curse-breaking prayer, which is different than a general prayer or a classic deliverance prayer, in that it specifically addresses the stronghold.

That evening the father of the child called the pastor back to his home. As the two sat down the father blurted out, "Could this be the work of a curse?" The pastor had not shared his insights with any of the family members. Now the man of God and the father were both wise to the root of the problem. The good news is, the little girl lived, and the women of this family feared no more because the curse had lost its power over this family.

A young couple I knew, fresh out of Bible School, were ministering in and around the Caribbean Islands in an area well known for the practices of voodoo, witchcraft, and curses. They were heavily involved in spiritual warfare. One afternoon as the husband was riding his motorbike down a country road, a horse that had been lazily grazing in a field suddenly jerked and headed for the fence. The crazed animal jumped the crude fence and landed squarely on the young minister, killing him instantly. Was this a freak accident? Did this happen by chance? Or could it have been a well-placed curse on a young man left unprotected through lack of intercession? I'm not sure, but it does make you stop and think.

Another bizarre experience, somewhat similar, took place in the state of Washington several years back. A pastor I knew, like many today, was researching the history of his city and area. He was looking for anything that gave evidence of demonic powers securing a beachhead or a stronghold, such as a broken covenant, violence, Masonic influence and the like. The pastor shared with his wife his excitement at a recent discovery he believed would blow a hole in the heavenlies – he believed he had located the regional strongman.

The next day he and a friend went canoeing on a local river. They paddled into sacred Indian waters. The pastor's canoe flipped, and though an excellent swimmer and former lifeguard, he drowned.

His wife contacted me soon after the tragedy. "Pastor Dick, where did he miss it?"

"I don't know," I sadly replied. "I just don't know."

Since these and other tragic experiences have come to my attention, I have become increasingly aware of the need for constant intercession on behalf of spiritual warriors. Any intrepid Christian or missionary who attempts to pull down a ruling prince had better be protected day and night. Other key attributes needed by such an individual would be personal holiness, unity in the home and the church, a heart free from bitterness, strife, envy or unforgiveness. Above all, I'm convinced that massive intercession is necessary.

One of the more interesting meetings I've held took place in Bend, Oregon. Bend is gorgeous, but, like all of Central Oregon, it's a hotbed of New Age activity. The invitation came through a pastor who invited me for a three-day spiritual warfare seminar. The first night, as I frequently do, I asked the people in the service to bring me books and articles on the history of Bend.

The next day the local pastor and his lovely wife invited me over for coffee and fellowship. I could feel tension in the atmosphere. I thought perhaps they were going through some difficulty, which is not unusual in the ministry.

The pastor's wife stared at me for a moment before asking, "Why are you here?"

The tone of her voice startled me momentarily. "Well, I am not sure why the Lord has me here, but I pray I can be a blessing and help to all of you," I responded adding, "But, I can't promise you anything."

With that, she burst into tears.

"Dear God in heaven, what did I say," I wondered?

After a few moments, she recovered her composure, "I'm sorry, Pastor Dick, but thank you for being the first honest speaker we've had in a long, long time." She went on to tell me a shocking story that both angered and frustrated me. Well-known evangelists had come to town and promised the moon, raised large amounts of money for future crusades and then never returned, and did not even make a phone call or send a letter. Promise-breaking preachers wore out the believers of Bend, Oregon.

Before the evening service, a sister asked if she could have a word with me. "Pastor Dick, I thought this might be of some interest to you. The local Indians used to call this place, *The Land of Broken Promises*." Apparently, the curse was still operating and even affecting good Christian ministers who fell under its power.

That night, I stood and prayed for every evangelist and pastor who had broken their word to these precious people, and begged forgiveness on their behalf. After much weeping and travailing, we experienced a joyous breakthrough.

The Bible and experiential reality both seem to suggest that corporate curses can be leveled against the inhabitants of particular territories. Here are some examples of curses directed at nations and cities.

> *The Lord had said to Abram: Get out of your country, from your kindred and from your father's house, to a land that I will show you. I will make you a great nation; I will bless you and make your name great, and you shall be a blessing. I will bless those who bless you, and I will curse him who curses you; and in you all the families of the earth shall blessed. (Genesis 12:1-3)*

I wonder how many nations and even empires have come to wish they had taken this passage seriously: "I will curse him (nations) who curses you (Israel).

In Lester Sumrall's book, *Jerusalem: Where Empires Die,* he pointed out how world powers have crumbled after tampering with the Holy Land and its capital city, Jerusalem. As far back as the Assyrian, Babylonian, Persian, Grecian, and Roman Empires, even up to this century, would-be conquerors have ruled over that land. From 1517 to 1917, the Turks (Ottoman Empire) controlled Palestine.

Shortly after World War I, the British and other allied troops seized Jerusalem without firing a shot. At that time England was a strong world power. The old saying still echoes in men's clubs throughout London today: "Remember, chaps when the sun never set on the British Empire?" But because of her mistreatment of Israel, England, like the empires before her, began to unwind. Around the late 1930's the country started declining from good to fair, to worse and things haven't fully recovered yet.

I pray America will continue to bless Israel and not reject her.

I know things get a little confusing because Israel doesn't always appear to act like a righteous nation, and the liberal humanists would love to turn on her. But let us remember this Psalm:

> *Many a time they have afflicted me from my youth: yet they have not prevailed against me. The plowers plowed on my back: they made their furrows long. The Lord righteous; He has cut in pieces the cords of the wicked. Let all those who hate Zion be put to shame and turned back; let them be as the grass on the housetops, which withers before it grows up, with which the reaper does not fill his hand, nor he who bind sheaves, his arms. Neither let those who pass by them say, 'The blessing of the Lord be upon you; we bless you in the name of the Lord.' (Psalm 129:1-8)*

One of the most interesting meetings we have had at Jubilee Christian Center took place when Loren Cunningham came and ministered on this subject. Loren, the founder of Youth With a Mission, brought some fascinating charts comparing the quality of life in certain nations. They touched on a wide spectrum of variables, from income, health, and longevity to their ability to feed people, the literacy rate, personal freedom and other areas. The charts came from a book he recommended, *Target Earth*, by a world missionary sharing valuable information for anyone who wants to see in living color the blessings of following Christ and, alternatively, the consequences of not following Him.

Using data from 131 nations and colored charts, Mr. Cunnigham compared the quality of life in the Christian nations to those in Islamic, Buddhist, Hindu, tribal-regulations, and non-religious countries – even in the Jewish nation of Israel. The difference is staggering. From the perspective he shared, it's clear we are following the right God and living by the right book.

It astounds me to think the New-Agers of America want to pull us into a religion based primarily on Hinduism and other Eastern mystical ideas. All it should take to squash this notion is a visit to India. My numerous missionary development deployments to India show the proof in the pudding. Take a good look at the cursed nation, India, which shows the fruit of demon worship.

Former Beatle, John Lennon, is well known for his hit song *Imagine,* the theme song and rally cry of the New World Order — the Age of Aquarius. The lyrics go something like this: *Imagine there's no heaven, it's easy if you try, no hell below us, above us only sky. Imagine all the people living for today. Imagine there's no countries, it isn't hard to do, nothing to kill or die for, and no religion too....*

I thought Karl Marx had sung that tune already, and look where it took his nation, as denoted in a 1990 national news publication that had a picture of a tombstone and the communist hammer and sickle on its cover with the title, *Death of a Nation USSR 1917.*

Shortly after this, I was reading an article in my local newspaper gushing over John Lennon and the world paying him homage, when I turned the page and came face-to-face with a picture of several poor Russian women, standing in the cold waiting hours to buy rotten apples. Yes, Russia imagined just what John Lennon sang about and became cursed because of it.

Thank God for the believers in Russia and the intercessors outside her boundaries who have prayed and continue to pray for change. It is obvious there are some believers in former communist countries who know something about spiritual warfare and curse breaking. We may need to import them to America if we don't act on our present problems quickly.

When the subject of spiritual warfare comes up in conversations, I often recommend the book, *Wrestling with Dark Angels.* This work is a collection of articles written by scholars and missionaries on the subject of strongholds, curses, and bondages that must be broken through prayer encounters. In it, Douglas Pennoyer wrote:

> *"Demonization is a personal relationship, the imposition of an evil spirit in the life of a human being. The Bible contains numerous accounts of demonization*

and personal case histories on the subject can be found in bookstores around the world. Much less attention has focused on the collective impact of demonized individuals in the society or subculture. We may be somewhat familiar with the classic manifestation of extreme individual demonization such as unusual strength, other voices, and disclosure of private information, but what are some of the features of the society or subculture with the majority of individuals are demonized?"

A curse can cause a whole society to come under demonic influence to one degree or another. If the society practices idol worship, it magnifies the problem. In the group of primitives Pennoyer worked with, he found some interesting key features of collective captivity. First was heavy demonization at the leadership level. These leaders were more likely controlled by strong, high-ranking territorial spirits of the region. The second thing he found, he referred to as demonic bonding — quoting Pennoyer:

Many individuals in the society or subculture are not only demonized but they have been bonded with their demons; this bond of friendship maybe especially strong generational or kin spirits were passed along family lines. The demon can reinforce this bond by acting as a family historian and reciting real or fabricated facts concerning the individual's ancestors.

Although Pennoyer's writings are based on his experiences with the Tawbuid people in the highlands of central

Philippines, don't for a minute think group demonization can't happen in civilized society. Satan's bag of tricks is the same for all cultures and societies regardless of country.

Ed Silvoso has identified what he called the five D's of warfare taken from a study of Exodus, chapters 1 and 2:

1. DECEPTION

    Satan, as the great deceiver, noticed that Pharaoh (a type of Satan) said in Exodus:

    "Come let us deal wisely with them, lest they multiply, and it happened, in the event of war, that they also join our enemies and fight against us, and so go up out of the land?" (Exodus 1:10)

    Pharaoh and Satan purposed to deal craftily to keep people in bondage.

2. DOMINATION

    "Therefore they set test taskmasters over them to afflict them with their burdens. And they built for Pharaoh supply cities, Pithom and Rameses." (Exodus 1:11)

    Pharaoh controlled them, and made them build the cities for them!

3. DISTRACTION

    "And he said, "When we do the duties of a midwife for the Hebrew women, and we see them on the birth stools if it is a son, then you shall kill him; but if it is a daughter then she shall live." (Exodus 1:16)

4. DIVINE & 5. DELIVERANCE

So God heard their groanings and God remembered his covenant with Abraham, with Isaac and with Jacob. And God looked upon the children of Israel and God acknowledged them. (Exodus 2:24-25)

God help us to convince nations that they are being deceived, dominated, and destroyed and that they must call upon the name of the Lord for divine deliverance. If they do not respond, they will have to reckon with God's warning in Leviticus:

Do not defile yourselves with any of these things; for by all these the nations are defiled, which I am casting out before you. For the land is defiled; therefore I visit the punishment of its iniquity upon it, and the land vomits out its inhabitants. (Leviticus: 18:24-25)

How many times have our hearts been broken by watching starving and afflicted people dying from famine and disease on a television newscast? We send offerings to ease our consciences, but the sufferers need much more than rice, milk, and a new tractor. They need curses broken off their nation!

The Bible is full of stories of cities that were cursed. Some were destroyed and never rebuilt; others repented and enjoyed a season of grace. Today, many modern cities are laboring under a curse unawares.

Once on my way to work, I was listening to talk radio news. The subject was, "Whatever happened to beautiful San

Francisco, one of America's showpieces, a world-class city, the Paris of the West?"

One caller, a dignified sounding gentleman with a bit of a British accent, talked about the good old days of the City by the Bay, back in the 50's and 60's when San Francisco was dotted with quaint little shops and restaurants. He remembered a time when people could take evening strolls without a panhandler or hooker bumping into them, a time when you didn't see the homeless sleeping in every doorway or taking up every park bench, a time when it was rare to see men kissing and openly fondling each other unashamedly in front of decent men, women and children.

The city that once had a surplus of funds is now hopelessly in debt. Indeed, liberals and homosexuals dictate many of the city's laws and policies. "No wonder tourism is down over fifty percent," the caller chimed in.

All this plus killer earthquakes, I thought to myself.

What has happened to beautiful San Francisco? The show's callers tried to put a finger on it. But I had an idea that most wouldn't have a clue about regarding San Francisco; San Francisco has been cursed! For all this, I've seen worse. All one has to do is tour Calcutta, New Delhi, Bombay or for that matter any city that has rejected Jesus Christ as Lord, and worships demons or self.

Recall Sodom and Gomorrah and how the stench of their sin got God's attention? Another major city, Nineveh, nearly suffered the same fate but heeded the words of the prophet

Jonah. Large portions of the books of Isaiah and Jeremiah focus on God's warning to Israel and other cities of Judah that curses would destroy them if they didn't turn back to their Lord.

> *Your country is desolate your cities are burned with fire; strangers devour your land in your presence and it is desolate, as over run by strangers. (Isaiah 1:7)*

Like many of you, I've traveled to the Holy Land several times to see, feel, and take in that wonderful, unique little strip of earth so destined by God. As much as I love Jerusalem and have many friends there, I have a real passion for Galilee. As we read the Gospels, we see a good deal of the Lord's ministry took place in and around this region. Whenever I tour Israel, one of the more significant cities we stop in is Capernaum. Unlike most other cities that were destroyed more than once, over the last 2,000 years, Capernaum has never rebuilt. Why? It sits in a very beautiful place.

Perhaps the answer lies in this passage:

> *Then He began to upbraid the cities in which most of His mighty works have been done, because they did not repent: Woe to you Chorazin! Woe to you Bethsaida! For if the mighty works which were done in you had been done In Tyre or Sidon, they would have repented long ago in sackcloth and ashes. But I say to you, it will be more tolerable for Tyre and Sidon in the Day of Judgment them for you. And you, Capernaum, who are exalted to heaven will be brought down to Hades; for if the mighty works which you were done in you had*

been done in Sodom, it would have remained until this day. But I say to you that it shall be more tolerable for the land of Sodom in the Day of Judgment than for you. (Matthew 11:20-24)

Many cities will not be won to the Lord unless the curses over them are understood and broken. The prophet Jeremiah received a strong word from the Lord about removing a curse before blessings would come:

Then the Lord put forth his hand and touched my mouth, and the Lord said to me, 'Behold I have put my words in your mouth. See I have this day set you over the nations and over the kingdoms to root out and to pull down, to destroy and throw down to build and to plant.' (Jeremiah 1:9-10)

The book of Joshua displays a biblical model for spiritual warfare. Indeed, Joshua conquered the Promised Land by taking one city at a time. For more details let me suggest John Dawson's book *Taking Our Cities For God*. Both deal in depth with the subject.

For several years our church hosted a spiritual warfare conference. On the final night of each conference, we concluded by taking thousands of believers to various places around San Jose and the South Bay Area to pray and break any curse holding God's blessings. We visited areas we knew to be strongholds and areas of influence and power. The results were amazing. I've encouraged many pastor friends to do the same and several major cities now have breakthrough nights.

God loves cities. The Bible is full of stories about cities. In fact, the greatest of all cities is being handcrafted right now by the Lord himself, the New Jerusalem, and will come down from heaven like a bride adorned for her husband.

REDEEMING THE LAND

One of my great pleasures in life is to meet wonderful servants of the Lord. I am blessed to call many of them my friends. One who had much experience with cursed land is Gwen Shaw. Sister Shaw had a ministry called End Time Handmaidens and is located in Jasper, Arkansas. A must for your library is her book *Redeeming the Land*. Gwen said that in order to break a curse off land, be it a nation, a city or just a piece of property, there are certain steps that should be followed:

First, share your burden with others. Get only courageous and strong intercessors that live a holy life and have faith to work with you. Unholy lives can be vulnerable to evil spirits. You'll be coming up against strong demon princes who have ruled over their areas for centuries, and your protection is your holy life, your faith, and the blood of Jesus. Then she shared:

- Prepare your hearts with prayer and fasting.
- Ask God to show you the area He wants you to go to. Locate national shrines, places where murder or suicide or innumerable violence or accidents have taken place and where witchcraft has been practiced.

- Go with the group, never alone!
- On arrival, begin to praise the Lord. Stay open to the Holy Spirit for further revelation about strongholds.
- Confess sins to the Lord on behalf of the transgressors. Bring everything into the light. Evil and demons do not like the light.
- Exalt the Lord with High Praises. Sing in the Spirit. Declare victory.
- Have Communion: *You prepare a table before me in the presence of my enemies. (Psalms 23:5)*
- Ask God to send the protecting angels to camp about you.
- Anoint the ground with oil.
- Prophesy life and blessing to the land.

A good way to close this particular type of curse-breaking ceremony, whether over land or people, is with spontaneous praise, joy, and even laughter in the Spirit. I've received many testimonies from folks all over the world who read one of my books, did what I suggested and saw it work. Droughts were broken, church splits averted, marriages saved, finances restored, children set free from drugs... You name it the curse can be broken.

" Victory belongs to those
   who believe in it the most,
   and believe in it the longest."

— *Randall Wallace*
   Screen Writer "Braveheart"

" War must be, while we
defend our lives against
a destroyer who would
devour all; but I do not
love the bright sword
for its sharpness, nor the
arrow for its swiftness,
nor the warrior for his
glory. I love only that
which they defend."
— *J.R.R. Tolkien*

CHAPTER 20

Christian Cursing

Like blessings, curses are a reality. The curse cleaves to the sinner, pursues him, hunts him down, ruins, and slays him. By experience:

> *"Rarely says Horace, 'has punishment through lame, failed to overtake the criminal fleeing before her.' By mythology: it was a conviction, true alike to conscience and the facts of life, which the Greeks sought to personify in the Erinyes, in Nemesis and in Ate, who clung to a man or to a family and punishment for some half forgotten crime; by literature which is full of recognition of avenging powers. The Bible confirms the substance of this varied teaching but lifts the subject out of the region of mythology." (Pulpits Commentary, The Book of Deuteronomy, MacDonald, publishing Co. pages 436-437)*

Curses figure prominently into pagan or heathen sorcery. A curse maybe placed by various means including charms, incantations, potions or mixtures of diverse ingredients (very strange ingredients I might add). In one city in Argentina, I was told of a witch who mixed oil and dirt from a graveyard to place a curse on the particular object or person. Also, during a visit to Omar Cabrera's Bible school, his wife, Marfa, took Larry Huggins and me to a spot where a few nights before spiritualists had come onto their property and placed a curse using candle ashes and other items. We broke the curse and cleansed the area in prayer, praise, and proclamation.

As Christians, we are appalled and offended at the very thought of placing a curse on another person. But the truth is that far too much witchcraft flourishes in churches today. What do I mean by witchcraft? I mean the spirit of control, manipulation, and domination. When the apostle Paul upbraided the Galatians church, he exclaimed, "Oh foolish Galatians who has bewitched you?" (Galatians 3:1). The word bewitched means *leading astray, misleading by an evil eye, working charms or to bring evil on a person by feigned praise.* Someone within the Galatian church had worked witchcraft. Paul went on later to declare:

> *For as many as are of the works of the law are under the curse, for it is written in 'Cursed is everyone who does not continue in all the things which are written in the in the book of the law, to do them. (Galatians 3:10)*

In other words, those who bewitched believers were cursed, and were trying to make others cursed as well. Paul felt so adamantly about the evil involved that in his opening remarks to his beloved Galatians he said:

"As we have said before if anyone preaches any other gospel to you then what you have received let him be accursed." (Galatians 1:9)

Accursed! The Greek word is *anathema*. Anyone or anything that attempts to nullify the death of Christ or preaches another way to the Father is to be given over to total destruction.

THE POWER OF WORDS

Evil manipulation doesn't have to involve crucial points of doctrine. Our day-to-day conversations and even our prayers can too often be laced with words phrased to control or manipulate others. The Bible offers both warning and advice in this regard:

But no man can tame the tongue. It is an unruly evil, full of deadly poison. With it we bless our God and Father, and with it we curse men, who have been made in the similitude of God. Out of the same mouth proceed blessing and cursing. My brethren, these things ought not to be so. Does a spring send forth fresh water and bitter from the same opening? Can a fig tree, my brethren, bear olives, or a grapevine bear figs? Thus no spring yields both salt water and fresh. Who is wise and understanding among you? Let him show by good conduct that his works are done in the meekness of wisdom. But if you have bitter envy and self-seeking in your hearts, do not boast and lie against the truth.

This wisdom does not descend from above, but is earthly, sensual, demonic. For where envy and self-seeking exist, confusion and every evil thing are there. But the wisdom that is from above is first pure, then peaceable, gentle, willing to yield, full of mercy and good fruits, without partiality and without hypocrisy. Now the fruit of righteousness is sown in peace by those who make peace. (James 3:8-18)

The power of words is a subject still in great need of research. In many ways, our lives are shaped and molded by words spoken over us. When children are told they will never amount to anything, that they are no good, they will then seek a way to fulfill that curse. On the other hand, a child who is encouraged, loved and blessed will usually grow up to be a blessing.

LEADERS BEWARE – BE ON GUARD!

The startling revelation is that the spirit world knows that Jesus has all the power and authority:

Now in the synagogue there was a man who had a spirit of an unclean demon. And he cried out with a loud voice, saying, "Let us alone! What have we to do with You, Jesus of Nazareth? Did You come to destroy us? I know who You are—the Holy One of God!" (Luke 4:33-34)

When He had come to the other side, to the country of the Gergesenes, there met Him two demon-possessed men, coming out of the tombs, exceedingly fierce, so that no one could pass that way. And suddenly they cried out, saying, "What have we to do with You, Jesus, You Son of God? Have You come here to torment us before the time?" (Matthew 8:28-29)

Also there were seven sons of Sceva, a Jewish chief priest, who did so. And the evil spirit answered and said, "Jesus I know, and Paul I know; but who are you?" (Acts 19:14-15)

The demons acknowledged Jesus as the Son of God. They tremble at His name, so there is no argument in the spirit world over the authority of Christ. This is why demons start to drool whenever a preacher of the gospel gives in to the flesh and becomes angry, jealous, hurt or threatened. If an evil spirit can get a follower of Jesus, especially an anointed leader with recognized authority, to curse a brother or sister through irresponsible words, the curse can be extremely potent.

It is no surprise and no big deal when the world brings an accusation against the believer. But when a respected minister writes a book defaming other ministries, the lid blows off the pressure cooker. This can result in church splits, arguments, more discord and plenty of confused Christians.

How many times have we heard evangelists or Pastors rail against another brother because he preaches slightly differently? One who comes to mind used to reference a brand of chewing tobacco when he would say publicly, "Copeland, Hagin — not Copenhagen. Chew it up and spit it out." I know that Kenneth Copeland and the late Kenneth

Hagin are two God-fearing people who have brought the body to the reality of strong faith. One may not agree with them on every point of doctrine, but the body has certainly had a great need for an understanding that God kind of faith.

Moreover, I have noticed that ministers who choose to curse in this manner, instead of having blessings, seem to suffer from financial problems, marriage problems, rebellious children, even premature death. Many fail to learn this or choose to ignore these truths:

> *Therefore you are inexcusable, O man, whoever you are who judge, for in whatever you judge another you condemn yourself; for you who judge practice the same things. But we know that the judgment of God is according to truth against those who practice such things. And do you think this, O man, you who judge those practicing such things, and doing the same, that you will escape the judgment of God? (Romans 2:1-3)*

THE WORD AS A WEAPON

The Bible not only enlightens us about potential grounds for being cursed, but it also provides a powerful weapon for breaking the hold of such curses.

> *My son… incline your ear to my saying. Do not let them depart from your eyes; keep them in the midst of your heart, for they are life to those who find them and health to all their flesh. (Proverbs 4:20-22)*

I put a high premium on quoting specific scriptures for specific problems. It is paramount when binding and losing to quote the Word of God with, *It is written*. Next are some profitable verses for dealing with potential curses. To break a curse, name it and apply the name of Jesus, His blood, and His word!

- **Alcoholism** – Joel 2:32, Psalm 107:6, II Corinthians 2:14
- **Uncontrollable Anger** – Proverbs 16:32; Proverbs 19:11, Ephesians 4:31
- **Fear** – Philippians 4:6-7; 1 Peter 5:7
- **Barrenness** – Deuteronomy 7:9-14; Psalm 113:9
- **Blood Disorders** – Proverbs 3:5-8; Hebrews 4:12; Joel 3:21
- **Cancer** – Proverbs 4:20-22; III John 2; James 5:16
- **Disease in General** – Jeremiah 17:14; Jeremiah 33:6; Psalm 107:20
- **Disorders of the Eyes and Ears** – Isaiah 32:3; Matthew 11:5
- **Insomnia** – Psalm 3:5; Psalm 4:8; Proverbs 3:24
- **Mental Health** – Psalm 25:17; Psalm 94:19; Proverbs 16:3
- **Poverty (Financial Problems)** – Psalm 34:9-10; Psalm 37:25; II Corinthians 8:9

THE CHRISTIAN'S GREATEST DEFENSE

Christians who are walking in righteousness and holiness need have no fear of the enemy. While we wage mortal combat against him, our adversary may aim a barrage of curses at us like heavy artillery. But although we may take hits occasionally, no evil can take root in those who abide in Christ and in His Word. A curse has no defense against God's Word!

No weapon formed against you shall prosper, and every tongue which rises against you in judgment you shall condemn. This is the heritage of the servants of the Lord, and their righteousness is from Me, says the Lord. (Isaiah 54:17)

" The two most
powerful warriors
are patience
and time."
— *Leo Tolstoy*

" I used to be
afraid of the
dark until I
learned I am
light, and now
the dark is
afraid of me."
— *Anonymous*

CHAPTER 21

Removing the Seven "'Ites" Off Your Promises

When the Lord your God brings you into the land which you go to possess, and has cast out many nations before you, the Hittites and the Girgashites and the Amorites and the Canaanites and the Perizzites and the Hivites and the Jebusites, seven nations greater and mightier than you, and when the Lord your God delivers them over to you, you shall conquer them and utterly destroy them. You shall make no covenant with them nor show mercy to them. (Deuteronomy 7:1-2)

The Promised Land was a land to be possessed, fought for, and occupied. God's promises to us must be claimed by faith!

In the book of Numbers God told Moses:

Now the Lord spoke to Moses in the plains of Moab by the Jordan, across from Jericho, saying, "Speak to the children of Israel, and say to them: 'When you have crossed the Jordan into the land of Canaan, then you shall drive out all the inhabitants of the land from before you, destroy all their engraved stones, destroy all their molded images, and demolish all their high places;" (Numbers 33:50-53)

Notice: first dispossess, then possess. These seven 'ites or strongholds had to be destroyed for Israel to fully claim God's promise to them. God's commands are not suggestions:

But if you do not drive out the inhabitants of the land from before you, then it shall be that those whom you let remain shall be irritants in your eyes and thorns in your sides, and they shall harass you in the land where you dwell. (Numbers 33:55)

All seven enemies must be dealt with. Leave even just one, and as the Bible says, *little leaven can ruin the whole lump.*

Who were these 'ites and what does that have to do with us today?

1. **Canaanites** – These were merchants and traders, unscrupulous sorts. Greedy and materialistic.
2. **Hittites** – These were horribly warlike and fierce people. The thought of them would instill fear into one's heart.
3. **Hivites** – Their name means *to live a lie.*
4. **Perizzites** – Unprotected, open, no walls, nomadic, restless people.
5. **Girgashites** – Dwellers of the clay or marsh.
6. **Amorites** – Mountain people, lived above the rest.
7. **Jebusites** – Trodden down, depressed.

SPIRIT OF MATERIALISM

If you're around my age you might remember the old tune that had the line, "Money, honey, if you want to get along with me," or the *Big Bopper* and his famous laugh line, "Oh Baby, you know what I like… *Money*."

Money – that strange stuff that turns the world's crank. Too much of it is dangerous, and so is too little. Where is the balance for the believer? Just how much is too much? Poverty is certainly not God's will, nor is decadence. Jesus came that we might have life, and have it more abundantly (John 10:10). But where does money come into this, or does it? Are God's blessings only spiritual, or is He also concerned with our natural needs?

We know the scripture:

> *For the love of money is a root of all kinds of evil, for which some have strayed from the faith in their greediness, and pierced themselves through with many sorrows. (1 Timothy 6:10)*

Paul did not say that money is evil, but our love for it is. Money is not immoral, but amoral. It's simply a tool, and what we do with this tool is being, and will be judged.

As a kid, I loved the Jack Benny Show. We would all gather around our black and white RCA television set and howl at Jack, Rodchester, Don, and Mary. One of my favorite skits had Jack being held up by a thug. The robber said, "Your money or your life!" Jack slowly looked into the camera and asked, "How long do I have to make up my mind?"

Sometimes during the offering at Jubilee, I see a few of the same blank expressions as God tries to deliver man from his money. Even though we sit on our wallet, it's still the object closest to our heart:

> For where your treasure is, there your heart will be also. (Matthew 6:21)

Jesus also tells us it's hard for the rich to enter heaven because too often their faith and love are wrapped up in their things. This doesn't pertain to all the rich, but a good majority of them.

One very successful businessman approached a famous preacher and told him, "Son, I'd sure like to help your ministry, but my money's all tied up." The preacher looked square at him and replied, "Sir, perhaps it's you who is all tied up?"

One of my favorite subjects to teach on is the subject of wisdom. The text I use is the book of Proverbs; it tells us in two-line poems how to live successfully on this planet. The key foundational words besides wisdom are instruction, integrity, discretion, understanding, knowledge, justice, prudence, and counsel. Once the foundation is laid, Solomon goes on to talk about the proper use of money. Here's a man who knows money's place. He compares the blessing and the cursing of riches. Basically, it depends on the person's heart and attitude towards money:

> He who has a slack hand becomes poor, but the hand of the diligent makes rich. (Proverbs 10:4)

> The spirit of a man will sustain him in sickness, but who can bear a broken spirit? The heart of the prudent

acquires knowledge, and the ear of the wise seeks knowledge. A man's gift makes room for him, and brings him before great men. The first one to plead his cause seems right, until his neighbor comes and examines him. Casting lots causes contentions to cease, and keeps the mighty apart. (Proverbs 18:14-18)

Solomon warns us about trusting in riches:

He who diligently seeks good finds favor, but trouble will come to him who seeks evil. He who trusts in his riches will fall, but the righteous will flourish like foliage. (Proverbs 11:27-28)

When I give my yearly teaching on giving as worship, I always touch on one of my favorite parables of Jesus:

And He also said to His disciples:

"There was a certain rich man who had a steward, and an accusation was brought to him that this man was wasting his goods. So he called him and said to him, 'What is this I hear about you? Give an account of your stewardship, for you can no longer be steward.' "Then the steward said within himself, 'What shall I do? For my master is taking the stewardship away from me. I cannot dig; I am ashamed to beg. I have resolved what to do, that when I am put out of the stewardship, they may receive me into their houses.' "So he called every one of his master's debtors to him, and said to the first, 'How much do you owe my master?' And he said, 'A hundred measures of oil.' So he said to him, 'Take

your bill, and sit down quickly and write fifty.' "Then he said to another, 'And how much do you owe?' So he said, A hundred measures of wheat. 'And he said to him, 'Take your bill, and write eighty.' "So the master commended the unjust steward because he had dealt shrewdly. For the sons of this world are more shrewd in their generation than the sons of light. "And I say to you, make friends for yourselves by unrighteous mammon, that when you fail, they may receive you into everlasting habitations. He who is faithful in what is least is faithful also in much; and he who is unjust in what is least is unjust also in much. "Therefore if you have not been faithful in the unrighteous mammon, who will commit to your trust the true riches? And if you have not been faithful in what is another man's, who will give you what is your own? "No servant can serve two masters; for either he will hate the one and love the other or else he will be loyal to the one and despise the other. You cannot serve God and mammon." (Luke 16:1-13)

At a glance, one might scratch his head and wonder at the words of Jesus:

- The unjust steward is being commended?
- Make friends with unrighteous mammon?
- When you fail?
- The sons of the world are more shrewd than the sons of light?

We should note that the three preceding parables were spoken to the Pharisees, but this one was spoken to His disciples (us).

This little story is not as complex or mysterious as some commentators would lead us to believe. The dramatic personae are not numerous. Here's a wealthy landowner who has an embezzler as a steward or manager. It's not that the steward was inept but rather irresponsible—a squanderer of his master's goods. He's busted and he's given notice of termination. The man panics!

"Oh my, what am I to do? I'm above digging ditches and too proud to beg." What a prince of a guy! He cleverly comes up with a solution. Before news spreads of his dismissal, he makes friends at his boss' expense. He cuts a couple of deals to insure his life after employment. In verse 8, his master catches him again, but this time he gets a different response. The master tips his hat to his ex-manager for his cleverness. "You little son of a gun; you got me again." (D.B. Version!)

Maybe the landowner got a good laugh at it. Perhaps the rich man got his wealth the same way, and it was payback time. The steward got fired anyway, but he made provision for himself along the way. He knew how to work the world's system—a system that's corrupt, lustful, greedy, and absolutely without principle—an unrighteous system that works for the unrighteous. A system where lying, cheating, and backbiting is the ladder used to get to the top.

Halfway through verse eight, Jesus looks at his own followers and says, "For the children of this world are more shrewd in their generation than the sons of light (church people)."

Ouch! What a rebuke. What's behind this saying of His? It's simple: The world has a system, and one hundred percent of the world's people play the game. Some play it better than others, so they prosper. God's Kingdom has a system. It's called tithes and offerings, yet less than twenty percent of His sons work the system. We seem to have more confidence in Dow Jones than in Jesus Christ!

Our security and investments feel better to us in the world's soil than in God's kingdom.

The unjust steward worked his system and his system worked for him. We seem to be somewhat confused. Jesus tells us, 'Make friends with money" (verse 9). Yes, even with the world's money or mammon. How does one make friends with money? By putting it in the hands of God.

Our Lord goes on to say if we can't be faithful with money, paying our bills, tithes, vows, and so forth, how then can we expect God Almighty to entrust us with true riches? What are true riches?

Spiritual gifts, ministry gifts, anointings, and favor are true riches, just to name a few.

It never ceases to amaze me how flaky people desire spiritual power. In verse 13 our Lord gets strong. In essence, He's saying to us, the church, if you're not willing to give to God, yet you call yourself a Christian, you're a liar. You are the worst kind of hypocrite. The real reasons you're not giving are your fear of lack and love of self. Giving is worship.

- Who do we love?
- Who do we serve?
- Who do we worship?

To me the whole thing about christians and money can be settled in Deuteronomy:

> ...then you say in your heart, "My power and the might of my hand have gained me this wealth." And you shall remember the Lord your God, for it is He who gives you power to get wealth, that He may establish His covenant which He swore to your fathers, as it is this day. (Deuteronomy 8:17)

I don't think God is all that concerned with our houses, cars, clothes or food. Let's live according to our means and conscience, but keep our eyes on the big picture. The world patiently waits for the gospel.

Spirit of materialism, be bound in Jesus' name!

" Until you know
that life is war,
you cannot
know what
prayer is for."
— *John Piper*

CHAPTER 22

Hittites – Spirit of Fear

The Hittites were a gnarly bunch. The very name brought a chill down the spine of a brave Hebrew, yet to take the land of promise, the Hittites had to be dealt with. No skirting around the issue. Fear would have to be conquered for victory to come.

"Fear not!" These are two of the most widely used words in the whole Bible. Why is fear such a problem? It's like our reactions to a neighbor we've had for years. You know, the one we don't like, but we've grown accustomed to anyway.

Fear is an emotion that is all too familiar. Perhaps Adam can be blamed. It was his first response to the fall in the garden:

Then the Lord God called to Adam and said to him, 'Where are you?" So he said, "I heard Your voice in the garden, and I was afraid because I was naked; and I hid myself." (Genesis 3:9-10)

Fear is faith's greatest obstacle for it breeds doubt, torment, confusion, double-mindedness, flight, and hate. Besides these, it fosters the greatest sin found in the church today — compromise.

The Berkeley Reference Dictionary says fear is: *Alarm and agitation caused by expectation or realization of danger. To be frightened, to suspect, timid, to be apprehensive.*

There is, of course, another fear that is healthy. The fear of the Lord. The Bible commands us to have it:

> *The fear of the Lord is the beginning of knowledge. (Proverbs 1:7)*

Here the word fear speaks of reverence, awe, and respect. Both fears motivate. One pushes away; the other draws to. The negative kind of fear is one great big stop sign on your road to destiny. Fear is the dread of losing something:

- Your precious life
- Your things
- Your reputation
- Maybe a relationship
- Your money

Fear has driven people to do crazy things, even commit murder or suicide. Fear takes no chances; it reasons away victory; it looks for the easy way out; it seeks the comfort zone.

Is it any wonder that we are to pray daily for boldness and courage? I personally know the gut-wrenching feeling of fear. It grips one's soul like a cold, steel vice and slowly tries to squeeze all the strength out. More than once, over the last thirty-seven years of pastoring, I have woken up in a cold sweat worrying about all that could go wrong.

Fear's best friend is worry. Worry is the constant rehearsing of all that could go wrong.

I don't know how many times I've turned on my night-light and opened the book of Psalms to fellowship a little with my friend, King David. As I read of his agony and distress in times of trouble, I track with him to victory in God. It's amazing the strength that leaps off the pages of Holy Writ:

For God has not given us a spirit of fear, but of power and of love and of a sound mind. (2 Timothy 1:7)

There is no fear in love; but perfect love casts out fear, because fear involves torment. But he who fears has not been made perfect in love. (1 John 4:18)

Be strong and of good courage, for to this people you shall divide as an inheritance the land which I swore to their fathers to give them. Only be strong and very courageous, that you may observe to do according to all the law which Moses My servant commanded you; do not turn from it to the right hand or to the left, that you may prosper wherever you go. This Book of the Law shall not depart from your mouth, but you shall meditate in it day and night, that you may observe to do according to all that is written in it. For then you will make your way prosperous, and then you will have good success. (Joshua 1:6-9)

Spirit of fear, be bound in Jesus' name!

" Christianity
agrees with
Dualism that
this universe
is at war."
— *C.S Lewis*

CHAPTER 23

Hivites – The Spirit of Compromise and Deception

What's worse than lying? It's to live a lie and believe it to be the truth. The Bible tells us the devil has deceived the whole world. The world here speaks of those outside the Body of Christ. The masses of blind humanity are being led by false religions, hopes, and dreams, all based on a lie:

> ...whose minds the god of this age has blinded, who do not believe, lest the light of the gospel of the glory of Christ, who is the image of God, should shine on the. (2 Corinthians 4:4)

> So the great dragon was cast out, that serpent of old, called the Devil and Satan, who deceives the whole world, he was cast to the earth, and his angels were cast out with him. (Revelation 12:9)

To be deceived is to be misled, tricked, duped or fooled. Here's a scripture that typifies the epitome of deception from Jeremiah:

Behold, you trust in lying words that cannot profit. Will you steal, murder, commit adultery, swear falsely, burn incense to Baal, and walk after other gods whom you do not know, and then come and stand before Me in this house which is called by My name, and say, We are delivered to do all these abominations'? "Has this house, which is called by My name, become a den of thieves in your eyes? Behold, I, even I, have seen it, says the Lord. But go now to My place which was in Shiloh, where I set My name at the first, and see what I did to it because of the wickedness of My people Israel. And now, because you have done all these works, says the Lord, and I spoke to you, rising up early and speaking, but you did not hear, and I called you, but you did not answer, therefore I will do to this house which is called by My name, in which you trust, and to this place which I gave to you and your fathers, as I have done to Shiloh. And I will cast you out of My sight, as I have cast out all your brethren-the whole posterity of Ephraim. Therefore do not pray for this people, nor lift up a cry or prayer for them, nor make intercession to Me; for I will not hear you." (Jeremiah 7:8-16)

I've sat in my office and heard stories and fantasies from well-meaning folks and wondered how they could get so far off base and believe they're in God's will. For the most part, they are good, church people, yet somehow a little deception got in and grew into the craziness that everyone could see but them. I guess we all know what it's like to be fooled and to believe in people who have tricked us.

I've been associated with a few slick snakes passing themselves off as spiritual people. To change the truth into a lie takes awhile. Satan likes to spoon-feed small doses of compromise. A little here, a little there, and eventually *"The little foxes destroy the vine."* Is it any wonder the belt that holds our armor secure is called the "belt of truth"? All the other parts hang upon the truth!

Look at this Psalm:

> *Blessed is the man who walks not in the counsel of the ungodly, nor stands in the path of sinners, nor sits in the seat of the scornful; but his delight is in the law of the Lord, and in His law he meditates day and night. He shall be like a tree planted by the rivers of water, that brings forth its fruit in its season, whose leaf also shall not wither; and whatever he does shall prosper. The ungodly are not so, but are like the chaff which the wind drives away. Therefore the ungodly shall not stand in the judgment, nor sinners in the congregation of the righteous. For the Lord knows the way of the righteous, but the way of the ungodly shall perish. (Psalm 1:1-6)*

Notice the sequence:

1. Walking
2. Standing
3. Sitting

Walk not in compromise, because if you do, you'll stop, and if you stop, you'll eventually sit. How many young christians started their walk right, but compromise crept in and got them off course? Notice the ungodly sinners and the scornful, and avoid them all!

King David wrote Psalm 51 out of brokenness. He had sinned against God by going into Bathsheba and eventually having Uriah, her husband, killed. Nathan, the prophet, rebuked the king. David could have lied to save his hide, blamed others for his sin, or even had Nathan killed for talking to the king that way. But no, David loved God and truth.

Integrity is tested more in bad times than in good times. How you and I handle mistakes will determine how we handle success. When God's instructions are crystal clear, we need not confer with flesh and blood. Everyone has an opinion, and they are quick to share it. Counsel is good, but not at the expense of the *royal command*. The Lord rarely chooses the path of least resistance.

- Speak the truth in love
- Walk the walk of truth
- Fight for truth

Spirit of compromise and deception, be bound in Jesus' name!

CHAPTER 24

Perizzites –
Spirit of Immorality

Flee sexual immorality. Every sin that a man does is outside the body, but he who commits sexual immorality sins against his own body. Or do you not know that your body is the temple of the Holy Spirit who is in you, whom you have from God, and you are not your own? For you were bought at a price; therefore glorify God in your body and in your spirit, which is God's.
(1 Corinthians 6:18)

Now concerning the things of which you wrote to me: It is good for a man not to touch a woman. Nevertheless, because of sexual immorality, let each man have his own wife, and let each woman have her own husband. Let the husband render to his wife the affection due her, and likewise also the wife to her husband. The wife does not have authority over her own body, but the husband does. And likewise the husband does not have authority over his own body, but the wife does. Do not deprive one another except with consent for a time that you may give yourselves to fasting and prayer; and come

> *together again so that Satan does not tempt you because of your lack of self control. But I say this as a concession, not as a commandment. (1 Corinthians 6:18-7:6)*

Ever notice that sexual sins are talked about more than any other in the Bible? God made us and gave us a sex drive. Sex was not created to be perverted, dirty, used as means to solely get physical satisfaction or to be sold. Sex is a celebration of love between covenant mates, not the culmination of lust. Love gives – lust takes. Love is humble and submissive; lust is arrogant and possessive. Lust is taking one's sex drive and putting it into overdrive. Immorality is not a new phenomenon. It's been around since time (man's time) began.

Homosexuality is not a San Francisco invention. It too has been around a long, long time. Venereal diseases of all kinds and perhaps even AIDS aren't new. The Bible speaks of such things as being a part of the curse. A recent CNN/Time poll said the decline in morality was the number two concerns of Americans, right behind violence. Interesting! Maybe America is waking up. The *love-ins* of the 60's and the *anything goes* of the 70's and 80's have soured in our mouths:

> *For the lips of an immoral woman drip honey and her mouth is smoother than oil; but in the end she is bitter as wormwood, sharp as a two-edged sword. Her feet go down to death, her steps lay hold of hell. Lest you ponder her path of life-her ways are unstable; you do not know them. (Proverbs 5:3-6)*

STD's, abortion-on-demand, rape, children out of wedlock,

and an assortment of other sexually related tragedies are placing a high demand on government dollars, not to mention social trauma. In America, six out of ten marriages end in divorce; many are a result of unfaithfulness. This 'ite has ruined many a good preacher, male and female. Paul spoke much about this, especially to the Corinthian church:

> It is actually reported that there is sexual immorality among you, and such sexual immorality as is not even named among the Gentiles that a man has his father's wife! (1 Corinthians 5:1)

> Foods for the stomach and the stomach for foods, but God will destroy both it and them. Now the body is not for sexual immorality, but for the Lord, and the Lord for the body. (1 Corinthians 6:13)

> Nevertheless, because of sexual immorality, let each man have his own wife, and let each woman have her own husband. (1 Corinthians 7:2)

> Nor let us commit sexual immorality, as some of them did, and in one day twenty-three thousand fell. (1 Corinthians 10:8)

Our senses are bombarded daily with sensual images: billboards, television, movies, music, dress and smell. It's impossible to isolate oneself from all of it, so we must pray for strength daily, or like the Perizzites, our walls will come down and we will be unprotected.

Spirit of immorality, be bound in Jesus' name!

" When we lift
our voice to
worship Jesus,
the devil
loses his."
— *Seth Dahl*

CHAPTER 25

Girgashites – Spirit of Double-Mindedness

But let him ask in faith, with no doubting, for he who doubts is like a wave of the sea driven and tossed by the wind. For let not that man suppose that he will receive anything from the Lord; he is a double-minded man, unstable in all his ways. (James 1:6-8)

I know your works, that you are neither cold nor hot. I could wish you were cold or hot. So then, because you are lukewarm, and neither cold nor hot, I will spew you out of My mouth. (Revelation 3:15-16)

The Girgashites were a type of gray-area-living church people, living by no real absolutes, no black or white. These folks floundered around in the pastels of life, stuck in the mud without enough sense to know it.

A friend of mine shared a story about a drunk driver who was fleeing from the cops. The drunk lost control of his vehicle and went into the grassy divider of the freeway. Since it had been raining, his tires quickly sank into the mud. The drunk floored the pedal, and the back tires simply spun and threw mud everywhere. The cops just watched and laughed until they handcuffed him. The drunk had the accelerator down, and the motor was revving, but he wasn't going anywhere:

> *I waited patiently for the Lord; and He inclined to me, and heard my cry. He also brought me up out of a horrible pit, out of the miry clay, and set my feet upon a rock, and established my steps. (Psalm 40:1-2)*

The muck and the mire are no place for the believer:

> *For if, after they have escaped the pollutions of the world through the knowledge of the Lord and Savior Jesus Christ, they are again entangled in them and overcome, the latter end is worse for them than the beginning. For it would have been better for them not to have known the way of righteousness, than having known it, to turn from the holy commandment delivered to them. But it has happened to them according to the true proverb: "A dog returns to his own vomit," and, a sow, having washed, to her wallowing in the mire." (2 Peter 2:20-22).*

Perhaps one's tendency to return to the swamps of life is because our bodies were formed of dust and clay, and with the Adamic nature constantly tempting and suggesting, some do slip. God is always there to rescue us.

Years ago a friend and I were going duck hunting in my four-wheel drive Ford pickup. We were almost to our destination when my friend needed to go to the bathroom. We were in the sticks with no gas stations in sight, so I just pulled off to the side of the road. Unfortunately, my truck slipped into a ditch.

No problem, I thought. I have four-wheel drive. To my surprise, I couldn't get out. I could go forward and backward in the wet ditch, but couldn't get out. We tried for two hours, getting more and more frustrated all the time. Finally, my friend walked to a nearby farm and got a man to bring his big tractor to pull us out. We needed more power than we had to get unstuck. We had someplace to go and something to do, so we didn't give up until we got out.

Don't give up. Get out of your ditch!

Spirit of double-mindedness, be bound in Jesus' name!

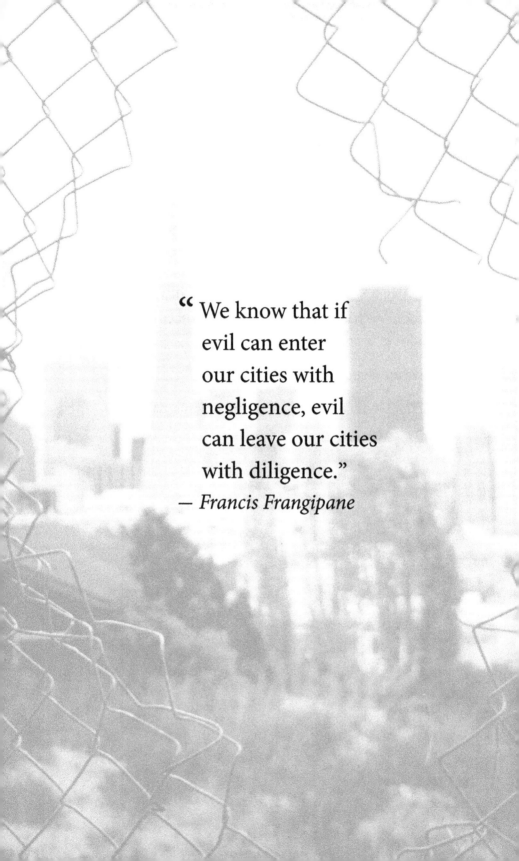

" We know that if
evil can enter
our cities with
negligence, evil
can leave our cities
with diligence."
— *Francis Frangipane*

CHAPTER 26

Amorites – Spirit of Pride

*And I said to you, You have come to the mountains
of the Amorites, which the Lord our God is giving us.
(Deuteronomy 1:20)*

The Amorites lived up in the mountains. According to Pastor
Maiden's research on these people, their very name means
proud, boastful, rebellious mountaineers. All through the
Old Testament, the Amorites were a real problem to the
Hebrew nation:

*But in the fourth generation they shall return here,
for the iniquity of the Amorites is not yet complete.
(Genesis 15:16)*

These arrogant dwellers of the Promised Land had very little
respect for the God of Israel. Too bad they never heard the
scripture, *"God resists the proud and gives grace to the humble."*
(James 4:6b).

But the children of God knew all too well how God
views pride:

I will set My face against you, and you shall be defeated by your enemies. Those who hate you shall reign over you, and you shall flee when no one pursues you. And after all this, if you do not obey Me, then I will punish you seven times more for your sins. I will break the pride of your power; I will make your heavens like iron and your earth like bronze. (Leviticus 26:17-19)

Pride is called the original sin, and it was the main cause of Lucifer's fall:

You were perfect in your ways from the day you were created, till iniquity was found in you. (Ezekiel 28:15)

How you are fallen from heaven, Lucifer, son of the morning! How you are cut down to the ground, you who weakened the nations! For you have said in your heart: "I will ascend into heaven, I will exalt my throne above the stars of God, I will also sit on the mount of the congregation on the farthest sides of the north; I will ascend above the heights of the clouds, I will be like the Most High." (Isaiah 14:12-14)

Pride says:

- I'll do it my way.
- I am self-sufficient.
- Get out of my way!

Simply put, pride is self-respect for one's own dignity, honor, and worth. Let me share a few proverbs with you:

I, wisdom, dwell with prudence, and find out knowledge and discretion. The fear of the Lord is to hate evil; pride and arrogance and the evil way and the perverse mouth I hate. (Proverbs 8:12-13)

Dishonest scales are an abomination to the Lord, but a just weight is His delight. When pride comes, then comes shame; but with the humble is wisdom. (Proverbs 11:1-2)

By pride comes only contention, but with the well advised is wisdom. (Proverbs 13:10)

Pride goes before destruction, and a haughty spirit before a fall. (Proverbs 16:18)

A man's pride will bring him low, but the humble in spirit will retain honor. (Proverbs 29:23)

Years ago I heard a television preacher boast that he was the only one preaching the whole truth. Not much later he fell and never recovered.

Recently, a friend and I were attending a minister's conference. A young, up-and-coming minister was firing away, taking pot shots at the faith movement, worship, spiritual warfare, and anyone or anything else that wasn't from his camp. My friend leaned over and whispered, "A couple of failures will humble that boy, and he'll be great as he grows."

Pride tells us:

- We're right, and others are wrong
- We can sin and get away with it
- We have to have more, bigger, faster, greater
- To rejoice in our brother's problems
- Not to forgive

Of the seven things that the Lord hates the most in Proverbs 6:16-19, pride is number one.

The Holy Spirit warns us in 1 John:

> *Do not love the world or the things in the world. If anyone loves the world, the love of the Father is not in him. For all that is in the world-the lust of the flesh, the lust of the eyes, and the pride of life-is not Of the Father but is of the world. And the world is passing away, and the lust of it; but he who does the will of God abides forever (1 John 2:15-17)*

Spirit of pride, be bound in Jesus' name!

CHAPTER 27

Jebusites –
Spirit of Depression

Here we meet and defeat the last of the seven 'ites. Depression, left unchecked, will lead to discouragement, despair, and condemnation. I read years ago the results of a poll taken in Newsweek Magazine indicating that one-third of all Americans are depressed, and the number of women who are depressed is on the rise.

Church people are not exempt from this attack. Life is a constant battle. Look at the many veterans wandering our city streets, depressed, mentally fatigued or battle weary.

Far too many of God's people have low self-esteem, weak faith, and battle condemnation daily.

Here's a favorite verse of mine:

> *And let us not grow weary while doing good, for in due season we shall reap if we do not lose heart. (Galatians 6:9)*

Many heroes of faith fought through depression and condemnation. Moses, Joshua, David, Elijah, Isaiah,

Jeremiah, and Peter all had their down times. Here are a few examples:

> *Then Joshua tore his clothes, and fell to the earth on his face before the ark of the Lord until evening, both he and the elders of Israel; and they put dust on their heads. And Joshua said, 'Alas, Lord God, why have You brought this people over the Jordan at all-to deliver us into the hand of the Amorites, to destroy us? Oh, that we had been content, and dwelt on the other side of the Jordan! "O Lord, what shall I say when Israel turns its back before its enemies? For the Canaanites and all the inhabitants of the land will hear it, and surround us, and cut off our name front the earth. Then what will You do for Your great name?" So the Lord said to Joshua: "Get up! Why do you lie thus on your face?" (Joshua 7:6-10)*

> *So David and his men came to the city, and there it was, burned with fire; and their wives, their sons, and their daughters had been taken captive. Then David and the people who were with him lifted up their voices and wept, until they had no more power to weep. And David's two wives, Ahinoam the Jezreelitess, and Abigail the widow of Nabal the Carmelite, had been taken captive. Then David was greatly distressed, for the people spoke of stoning him because the soul of all the people was grieved, every man for his sons and his daughters. But David strengthened himself in the Lord his God. (1 Samuel 30:3-6)*

And Ahab told Jezebel all that Elijah had done, also how he had executed all the prophets with the sword. Then Jezebel sent a messenger to Elijah, saying, "So let the gods do to me, and more also, if I do not make Your life as the life of one of them by tomorrow about this time." And when he saw that, he arose and ran for his life, and went to Beersheba, which belongs to Judah, and left his servant there. But he himself went a day's journey into the wilderness, and came and sat down under a broom tree. And he prayed that he might die, and said, "It is enough! Now, Lord, take my life, for I am no better than my fathers!" (1 Kings 19:1-4)

The problem with condemnation is that it feels much like conviction. Both have drawing power. Condemnation draws you away from God while conviction draws you to God. One is designed to destroy, the other to save.

Depression kills:

- Vision
- Hope
- Strength
- Zeal
- Joy

The literal meaning of Jebusite is *trodden down*. The devil wants to walk all over us, then stomp us into an early grave. A good friend of ours committed suicide some time go. He was a successful surgeon who appeared to have little want. He was a leader in his church and seemed content in life. He had mentioned his struggles with depression several years earlier but said he was doing much better now. Two months later he took his life. To this day we still shake our heads in disbelief. Why? Could we have helped? Was he reaching out to us? We almost allowed his depression to rub off on us.

In 1984, I had a miserable bout with depression. I laid on my couch for a week with thoughts of leaving the ministry. "It's too hard! Who needs all this grief! Who cares, anyway?" Boy, I had a Job-type of a pity party. My wife and a preacher friend encouraged me until I was back on my feet again. Today it's hard to get me down; I just don't let my guard down.

> *There is therefore now no condemnation to those who are in Christ Jesus, who do not walk according to the flesh, but according to the Spirit. For the law of the Spirit of life in Christ Jesus has made me free from the law of sin and death. For what the law could not do in that it was weak through the flesh, God did by sending His own Son in the likeness of sinful flesh, on account of sin: He condemned sin in the flesh. (Romans 8:1-3)*

Spirit of depression, be bound in Jesus' name!

CONCLUSION

There they are! The seven 'ites God warned the children of Israel about. Seven enemies that had to be dealt with before full victory could be enjoyed:

- Materialism
- Fear
- Compromise and Depression
- Immorality
- Double-mindedness
- Pride
- Depression

Any one of the seven can knock us out of the race or push us back into the wilderness. We are to know our enemy.

" In opposition to all the suggestions of the devil, the sole, simple, and sufficient answer is the Word of God."

— *Charles Hodge*

CHAPTER 28

Demons by Name

Then they came to the other side of the sea, to the country of the Gadarenes. And when He had come out of the boat, immediately there met Him out of the tombs a man with an unclean spirit, who had his dwelling among the tombs; and no one could bind him, not even with chains, because he had often been bound with shackles and chains. And the chains had been pulled apart by him, and the shackles broken in pieces; neither could anyone tame him. And always, night and day, he was in the mountains and in the tombs, crying out and cutting himself with stones. When he saw Jesus from afar, he ran and worshiped Him. And he cried out with a loud voice and said, "What have I to do with You, Jesus, Son of the Most High God? I implore You by God that You do not torment me." For He said to him, "Come out of the man, unclean spirit!" Then He asked him, "What is your name?" And he answered, saying, "My name is Legion; for we are many." (Mark 5:1-90)

This poor soul was a real trophy for Satan. He was a raving madman — tormented, screaming, howling, cutting himself, way strong, and living among the dead. What a wounded soul! Today, he would be in a straight jacket, locked up in a place for the insane. What interests me in this story is how, at the very sight of the approaching Christ, the man runs to Him and worships Him. Did he have a moment of clarity and somehow got the revelation of who this was? Is it simply Satan was still traumatized by the defeat he experienced in the wilderness while desperately trying to tempt Jesus?

Obviously, the demons are using the man's voice. They acknowledge him as Elion (most high God). Elion was the name of God used by the Phoenicians, and other neighboring nations bordering Israel. Maybe it's a hint as to where they came from; the demon(s) begged not to be tormented. This could mean, "Please don't send us to the abyss. We know we are doomed but Jesus, please, not yet."

In verse 8, Jesus commands the unclean spirit to come out. It didn't obey right away, so Jesus asks, "What is your name?" Every angel has a name. Every fallen angel has a name. They answered, "Legion, for we are many."

A Roman army (Legion) would usually consist of 6,000 men. Some suggested there were 2,000. Nonetheless, it was a lot.

A legion also implies that they were fully armed and ready for war. It's a military term. It's no wonder this poor soul was so vexed!

Also he begged Him earnestly that He would not send them out of the country. Now a large herd of swine was feeding there near the mountains. So all the demons begged Him, saying, "Send us to the swine, that we may enter them." (Mark 5:10-12)

Verse 10 gives us a peek into the strategy of Satan. They were territorial spirits. They begged not to be evicted from their territory. To the point, they preferred to be cast into pigs than have to leave their country's side (Verses 11-12).

Swine (pigs) are at the top of the list of unclean animals, according to the Law of Moses. Certain Jews raised pigs to feed the local Roman soldiers. This, of course, brought on disgust from the devout Jews who lived by the law. Jesus was always teaching and demonstrating to his disciples, and to others in the crowds who followed Him, that hell was no match for heaven. He allowed Legion to enter the pigs (Verses 13-17).

With the loss of two thousand pigs, which was significant, the locals asked Jesus to leave. Money was more important to them than heaven, even with the Son of God in their midst. Some things haven't changed much since then.

BEELZEBUB

Then one was brought to Him who was demon-possessed, blind and mute; and He healed him, so that the blind and mute man both spoke and saw. And all the multitudes were amazed and said, "Could this be the Son of David?" Now when the Pharisees heard it they said, "This fellow does not cast out demons except by Beelzebub, the ruler of the demons." But Jesus knew their thoughts, and said to them: "Every kingdom divided against itself is brought to desolation, and every city or house divided against itself will not stand. If Satan casts out Satan, he is divided against himself. How then will his kingdom stand? And if I cast out demons by Beelzebub, by whom do your sons cast them out? Therefore they shall be your judges. But if I cast out demons by the Spirit of God, surely the kingdom of God has come upon you." (Matthew 12:22-28)

Jesus came "to destroy the works of the devil." This soul in our text is suffering because of Satan's works. Let's be clear, all the strength of hell is no match for the strongest of the strong, Jesus! The Pharisees were familiar with the name Beelzebub. So was Jesus.

Just who is Beelzebub? Who is this ruler and prince of demons? His name means *dung god* or *lord of the flies*. It's probably just another name for Satan, the *master of darkness*. Another name that frequently pops up in the Old Testament and once in the New Testament is *Belial*.

Do not be unequally yoked together with unbelievers. For what fellowship has righteousness with lawlessness? And what communion has light with darkness? And what accord has Christ with Belial? Or what part has a believer with an unbeliever? And what agreement has the temple of God with idols? For you are the temple of the living God. As God has said: "I will dwell in them and walk among them. I will be their God. And they shall be my people." (2 Corinthians 6:14-16)

Belial means *wicked and worthless*. When the Bible speaks of the sons or children of Belial, it's talking about wicked, profane humans under demonic influence — criminals, murders, rapist, pedophiles, and such.

Getting back to Beelzebub, I tell people in my conferences, "If you want to understand the trafficking of demons, watch flies. They are attracted to corruption or waste (dung-god) — garbage, dried blood, dead animals, or anything or anywhere they can feast and lay their eggs and breed maggots. They swarm, and they use the atmosphere to move around." I like to say that the word of God is the ultimate fly swatter.

Another interesting name found in the Bible, is *Wormwood*.

Then the third angel sounded: And a great star fell from heaven, burning like a torch, and it fell on a third of the rivers and on the springs of water. 11 The name of the star is Wormwood. A third of the waters became wormwood, and many men died from the water, because it was made bitter (Revelations 8:10-11)

Wormwood means *toxic, bitter, poisonous or accursed*.

Who this star is, we don't know. Some suggest a political leader or false prophet or some great person of global influence corrupted by the *spirit of wormwood*. We, of course, know satan possessed a beautiful serpent in the garden to beguile our parents, but here, in the next text, we see demons appear somewhat like locust, another swarming pest!

Then the fifth angel sounded: And I saw a star fallen from heaven to the earth. To him was given the key to the bottomless pit. And he opened the bottomless pit, and smoke arose out of the pit like the smoke of a great furnace. So the sun and the air were darkened because of the smoke of the pit. Then out of the smoke locusts came upon the earth. And to them was given power, as the scorpions of the earth have power. They were commanded not to harm the grass of the earth, or any green thing, or any tree, but only those men who do not have the seal of God on their foreheads. And they were not given authority to kill them, but to torment them for five months. Their torment was like the torment of a scorpion when it strikes a man. In those days men will seek death and will not find it; they will desire to die, and death will flee from them. The shape of the locusts was like horses prepared for battle. On their heads were crowns of something like gold, and their faces were like the faces of men. They had hair like women's hair, and their teeth were like lions' teeth. And they had breastplates like breastplates of iron, and the sound of their wings was like the sound of chariots with many horses running into battle. They had tails like scorpions, and there were stings in their tails. Their power was to hurt men five months. And they had as king over them the angel of the bottomless pit, whose name in Hebrew is Abaddon, but in Greek, he has the name Apollyon. (Revelations 9:1-11)

This *fallen* star seems to be the antichrist to come. The final one! Notice how they look like an army ready for battle. Crowns representing false authority (fools gold), faces like men, hair like women, and teeth like a lion. They even have wings and a scorpion's tail. What a sight! But fear not dear ones, we will prevail.

Here are two more of his (the anti-Christ's) names Abaddon and Apollyon. Their meaning simply is *to destroy*. Satan comes but to kill, steal and destroy.

Idolatry was and is still prevalent in a big part of the world. All through the Old Testament, it posed a major problem for the Hebrews, and even in Paul's day the Greeks and Romans were extremely superstitious and idolatrous:

Therefore, my beloved, flee from idolatry. I speak as to wise men; judge for yourselves what I say. The cup of blessing which we bless, is it not the communion of the blood of Christ? The bread which we break, is it not the communion of the body of Christ? For we, though many, are one bread and one body; for we all partake of that one bread. Observe Israel after the flesh: Are not those who eat of the sacrifices partakers of the altar? What am I saying then? That an idol is anything, or what is offered to idols is anything? Rather, that the things which the Gentiles sacrifice they sacrifice to demons and not to God, and I do not want you to have fellowship with demons. (1 Corinthians 10:14-20)

Satan, and his demonic cadre love to be worshiped. They would possess idols made of wood or stone or even precious metals. As poor ignorant people would bring sacrifices, sing, dance, and chant, the powers of darkness would puff up with pride. An idol, of course, has names!

BAAL & ASHERAH

Then Elijah said, "As the Lord of hosts lives, before whom I stand, I will surely present myself to him today." So Obadiah went to meet Ahab, and told him; and Ahab went to meet Elijah. Then it happened, when Ahab saw Elijah, that Ahab said to him, "Is that you, O troubler of Israel?" And he answered, "I have not troubled Israel, but you and your father's house have, in that you have forsaken the commandments of the Lord and have followed the Baals. Now therefore, send and gather all Israel to me on Mount Carmel, the four hundred and fifty prophets of Baal, and the four hundred prophets of Asherah, who eat at Jezebel's table." (1 Kings 18:15-19)

DAGON

Then the Philistines took the ark of God and brought it from Ebenezer to Ashdod. When the Philistines took the ark of God, they brought it into the house of Dagon and set it by Dagon (1 Samuel 5:1-2)

MOLECH

Then the Lord spoke to Moses, saying, "Again, you shall say to the children of Israel: 'Whoever of the children of Israel, or of the strangers who dwell in Israel, who gives any of his descendants to Molech, he shall surely be put to death. The people of the land shall stone him with stones. I will set My face against that man, and will cut him off from his people, because he has given some of his descendants to Molech, to defile My sanctuary and profane My holy name." (Leviticus 20:1-3)

RIMMON

So Naaman said, "Then, if not, please let your servant be given two mule-loads of earth; for your servant will no longer offer either burnt offering or sacrifice to other gods, but to the Lord. Yet in this thing may the Lord pardon your servant: when my master goes into the temple of Rimmon to worship there, and he leans on my hand, and I bow down in the temple of Rimmon. When I bow down in the temple of Rimmon, may the Lord please pardon your servant in this thing." (2 Kings 5:17-18)

DIANA

"So not only is this trade of ours in danger of falling into disrepute, but also the temple of the great goddess Diana may be despised and her magnificence destroyed, whom all Asia and the world worship." Now when they heard this, they were full of wrath and cried out, saying, "Great is Diana of the Ephesians!" (Acts 19:27-28)

SUN, MOON & STARS

And the king commanded Hilkiah the high priest, the priests of the second order, and the doorkeepers, to bring out of the temple of the Lord all the articles that were made for Baal, for Asherah, and for all the host of heaven; and he burned them outside Jerusalem in the fields of Kidron, and carried their ashes to Bethel. Then he removed the idolatrous priests whom the kings of Judah had ordained to burn incense on the high places in the cities of Judah and in the places all around Jerusalem, and those who burned incense to Baal, to the sun, to the moon, to the constellations, and to all the host of heaven. And he brought out the wooden image from the house of the Lord, to the Brook Kidron outside Jerusalem, burned it at the Brook Kidron and ground it to ashes, and threw its ashes on the graves of the common people. Then he tore down the ritual booths of the perverted persons[d] that were in the house of the Lord, where the women wove hangings for the wooden image. (2 Kings 23:4-7)

It's interesting to me how even today we have products named after ancient gods such as:

Nike – winged goodness of victory
Mercury – the winged foot god of messages
Mazda – god of Asian wisdom
Hermes – Olympians god, son of Zeus

This is just a sampling of modern products we wear, drive, read, or have. Now, I'm not throwing away my Nike running shoes, my wife's purse, or my morning Mercury newspaper. Nor am I suggesting you sell your Mazda. My point is how names are still around and still with some significance. Someone said, "Well, here in sophisticated America we don't have idols." I would argue yes, we do: Movie idols, rock idols, sports idols, or anything that has our heart, our affection, our money and time is an object of devotion, simply put, is a 21st-century idol.

" Anxiety does not
empty tomorrow
of its sorrow, but
only empties today
of its strength."
— *Charles H. Spurgeon*

CHAPTER 29

Familiars

You shall keep My Sabbaths and reverence My sanctuary: I am the Lord. 'Give no regard to mediums and familiar spirits; do not seek after them, to be defiled by them: I am the Lord your God. (Leviticus 19:30-31)

These types of demons are called familiars. The word familiar tells us a lot about their modus operandi. Familiar means *acquainted with, intimate or personal*. I call them family spirits or familiar spirits. God views these spirits so dangerously that he told Moses:

"A man or a woman who is a medium, or who has familiar spirits, shall surely be put to death; they shall stone them with stones. Their blood shall be upon them." (Leviticus 20:27)

Then and even now we have mediums, fortunetellers, and psychics who traffic in this kind of spirit. Séances and Ouija boards can also attract familiar (family) spirits who have knowledge or information about deceased loved ones or even imitates someone who has passed away. We even have celebrity psychics who commune with the dead.

King Saul lost his kingdom messing around with a medium:

> "Now it happened in those days that the Philistines gathered their armies together for war, to fight with Israel. And Achish said to David, "You assuredly know that you will go out with me to battle, you and your men." So David said to Achish, "Surely you know what your servant can do." And Achish said to David, "Therefore I will make you one of my chief guardians forever." Now Samuel had died, and all Israel had lamented for him and buried him in Ramah, in his own city. And Saul had put the mediums and the spiritists out of the land. Then the Philistines gathered together, and came and encamped at Shunem. So Saul gathered all Israel together, and they encamped at Gilboa. When Saul saw the army of the Philistines, he was afraid, and his heart trembled greatly. And when Saul inquired of the Lord, the Lord did not answer him, either by dreams or by Urim or by the prophets. Then Saul said to his servants, "Find me a woman who is a medium, that I may go to her and inquire of her." And his servants said to him, "In fact, there is a woman who is a medium at En Dor." So Saul disguised himself and put on other clothes, and he went, and two men with him; and they came to the woman by night. And he said, "Please conduct a séance for me, and bring up for me the one I shall name to you." (1 Samuel 28:1-8)

Desperation often leads to stupidity or worse!

"Then the woman said to him, "Look, you know what Saul has done, how he has cut off the mediums and the spiritists from the land. Why then do you lay a snare for my life, to cause me to die?" And Saul swore to her by the Lord, saying, "As the Lord lives, no punishment shall come upon you for this thing." Then the woman said, "Whom shall I bring up for you?" And he said, "Bring up Samuel for me." When the woman saw Samuel, she cried out with a loud voice. And the woman spoke to Saul, saying, "Why have you deceived me? For you are Saul!" And the king said to her, "Do not be afraid. What did you see?" And the woman said to Saul, "I saw a spirit ascending out of the earth." So he said to her, "What is his form?" And she said, "An old man is coming up, and he is covered with a mantle." And Saul perceived that it was Samuel, and he stooped with his face to the ground and bowed down. Now Samuel said to Saul, "Why have you disturbed me by bringing me up?" And Saul answered, "I am deeply distressed; for the Philistines make war against me, and God has departed from me and does not answer me anymore, neither by prophets nor by dreams. Therefore I have called you, that you may reveal to me what I should do." Then Samuel said: "So why do you ask me, seeing the Lord has departed from you and has become your enemy? And the Lord has done for Himself as He spoke by me. For the Lord has torn the kingdom out of your hand and given it to your neighbor, David. (1 Samuel 28:9-17)

We dare not think we know all the mysteries at work here; how she did this, or what incantations she used. The fact is this is a familiar spirit, not the real Samuel. God would never allow a heathen witch to conjure up a great prophet. He looked like Samuel, talked like Samuel even told the truth, but this is a familiar spirit, not the real deal.

Years ago Carla and I performed deliverance on a family member who had foolishly attended a séance and even invited spirits to enter her. They did enter her and it was warfare getting them out. Thank God, we succeeded and our relative is fine to this day.

A friend of mine, back in the early sixties, consulted an Ouija board asking, "What is my real father's first name?" He was a foster kid, then in his late twenties. The board spelled out "Allen." He later found out that was the truth. The devil often tells the truth if it can get him an advantage. However, truth – real truth – is found in Christ and in him only!

CHAPTER 30

The High Places

And the princes of Moab rose and went to Balak, and said, "Balaam refuses to come with us." (Numbers 22:14)

In the twenty-seventh year of Jeroboam king of Israel, Azariah the son of Amaziah, king of Judah, became king. He was sixteen years old when he became king, and he reigned fifty-two years in Jerusalem. His mother's name was Jecholiah of Jerusalem. And he did what was right in the sight of the Lord, according to all that his father Amaziah had done, except that the high places were not removed; the people still sacrificed and burned incense on the high places. (2 Kings 15:1-4)

For we wrestle not against flesh and blood, but against principalities, against powers, against the rulers of the darkness of this world, against spiritual wickedness in high places. (Ephesians 6:12 - KJV)

For the weapons of our warfare are not carnal but mighty in God for pulling down strongholds, casting down arguments and every high thing that exalts itself against the knowledge of God, bringing every thought into captivity to the obedience of Christ, and being ready to punish all disobedience when your obedience is fulfilled. (2 Corinthians 10:4-6)

What are *high places?* Simply put they are an atmosphere that has been erected that is now creating high things! Things, thoughts, actions, and deeds that exalt themselves against God and His word, all these things have to be rooted out and broken.

In the Old Testament, there is a recurring theme of kings who, for the most part, did "Right in the sight of the Lord" but did not remove the *high places* of idol worship. This all started after Solomon's reign:

And Rehoboam the son of Solomon reigned in Judah. Rehoboam was forty-one years old when he became king. He reigned seventeen years in Jerusalem, the city which the Lord had chosen out of all the tribes of Israel, to put His name there. His mother's name was Naamah, an Ammonitess. Now Judah did evil in the sight of the Lord, and they provoked Him to jealousy with their sins which they committed, more than all that their fathers had done. For they also built for themselves high places, sacred pillars, and wooden images on every high hill and under every green tree. And there were also perverted persons in the land. They did according to all the abominations of the nations which the Lord had cast out before the children of Israel. (1 King 14:21-24)

David's grandson, the son of Solomon does evil and unrighteousness. Solomon unwisely marries Naamah, which means a *beauty*. She was an Amonite, not a Jewess.

Obviously, her traditions, culture, and religion had a strong influence over her son Rehoboam.

We must be careful not to be unequally yoked. Rehoboam allowed pagan worship and idolatry to flourish. He should have read the 28th chapter of Deuteronomy or at least remembered the 1st commandment given to Moses. And God spoke all these words, saying:

> *I am the Lord your God, who brought you out of the land of Egypt, out of the house of bondage. You shall have no other gods before Me. You shall not make for yourself a carved image—any likeness of anything that is in heaven above, or that is in the earth beneath, or that is in the water under the earth; you shall not bow down to them nor serve them. For I, the Lord your God, am a jealous God, visiting the iniquity of the fathers upon the children to the third and fourth generations of those who hate Me, but showing mercy to thousands, to those who love Me and keep My commandments. (Exodus 20:1-6)*

This breach of covenant promises brought this on:

> *It happened in the fifth year of King Rehoboam that Shishak king of Egypt came up against Jerusalem. And*

he took away the treasures of the house of the Lord and the treasures of the king's house; he took away everything. He also took away all the gold shields which Solomon had made. (1 Kings 14:25-26)

As long as high places were left intact, God held back His blessings. Every now and then a righteous King would arise and fully obey the word of the Lord and King, like young Josiah:

Josiah was eight years old when he became king, and he reigned thirty-one years in Jerusalem. His mother's name was Jedidah the daughter of Adaiah of Bozkath. And he did what was right in the sight of the Lord, and walked in all the ways of his father David; he did not turn aside to the right hand or to the left. (2 Kings 22:1-2)

And let them deliver it into the hand of those doing the work, who are the overseers in the house of the Lord; let them give it to those who are in the house of the Lord doing the work, to repair the damages of the house — to carpenters and builders and masons — and to buy timber and hewn stone to repair the house. However there need be no accounting made with them of the money delivered into their hand, because they deal faithfully. Then Hilkiah the high priest said to Shaphan the scribe, "I have found the Book of the Law in the house of the Lord." And Hilkiah gave the book to Shaphan, and he read it. (2 Kings 22:5-8)

But as for the king of Judah, who sent you to inquire of the Lord, in this manner you shall speak to him, Thus says the Lord God of Israel: "Concerning the words which you have heard; because your heart was tender, and you humbled yourself before the Lord when you heard what I spoke against this place and against its inhabitants, that they would become a desolation and a curse, and you tore your clothes and wept before Me, I also have heard you," says the Lord. "Surely, therefore, I will gather you to your fathers, and you shall be gathered to your grave in peace; and your eyes shall not see all the calamity which I will bring on this place." So they brought back word to the king. (2 Kings 22:18-19)

Here was a man who understood spiritual warfare, even back then. Unfortunately, Josiah was a rarity. It was much easier for Hilkiah to be tolerant of, accept, even celebrate, different forms of worship. At all cost, please the people. Let them do what they feel is right. Sounds like America today!

In our passion for *rights* and *acceptance*, we have erected new *high places*, which are welcome mats for demons. The word altar literally means *a raised* or *high place*. Of course, the word altar is the highest of the high. In the Old Testament, the brazen altar of the Lord was built on a mound. The priests would *go up to the altar.*

Paul tells us to "Pull down strongholds". Strongholds come from, and are formed in high places. The modern world has many institutions or places where strongholds are birthed, fed, and grow stronger: Godless families (parents), abortion clinics (Planned Parenthood), secular universities, and places of worship where the truth of Christ is maligned or non-existent, seats of power where laws are passed (despite the voting of God-fearing people) that ultimately slap God in the face. History proves all great past empires collapsed from the *rot within.*

So, what do we do?

Then the Lord appeared to Solomon by night, and said to him: "I have heard your prayer, and have chosen this place for Myself as a house of sacrifice. When I shut up heaven and there is no rain, or command the locusts to devour the land, or send pestilence among My people, if My people who are called by My name will humble themselves, and pray and seek My face, and turn from their wicked ways, then I will hear from heaven, and will forgive their sin and heal their land. Now My eyes will be open and My ears attentive to prayer made in this place. For now, I have chosen and sanctified this house, that My name may be there forever; and My eyes and My heart will be there perpetually" (2 Chronicles 7:12-16)

The battle is the Lord's! Our job is to pray (first things first), preach, witness, disciple, love, help, serve, give, and never stop praising His name.

CHAPTER 31

A City for the Taking!

After the death of Moses the servant of the Lord, it came to pass that the Lord spoke to Joshua the son of Nun, Moses' assistant, saying: "Moses My servant is dead. Now therefore, arise, go over this Jordan, you and all this people, to the land which I am giving to them—the children of Israel. Every place that the sole of your foot will tread upon I have given you, as I said to Moses." (Joshua 1:1-3)

"Be strong and of good courage, for to this people you shall divide as an inheritance the land which I swore to their fathers to give them. Only be strong and very courageous, that you may observe to do according to all the law which Moses My servant commanded you; do not turn from it to the right hand or to the left, that you may prosper wherever you go. This Book of the Law shall not depart from your mouth, but you shall meditate in it day and night, that you may observe to do according to all that is written in it. For then you will make your way prosperous, and then you will have

good success. Have I not commanded you? Be strong
and of good courage; do not be afraid, nor be dismayed,
for the Lord your God is with you wherever you go."
(Joshua 1:6-9)

After forty years of wilderness training, God's people were
ready to take a city. Moses led the Children of God for forty
years — a full generation! Then came the time when his time
and ministry was over. Moses died. It was the time for new
leadership, a new strategy, and a fresh anointing.

We should be thankful and grateful for our spiritual
forefathers of our regions, cities, and states who plowed and
prayed for revival. Their time was valuable and blessed but
like Moses' time in the desert, over.

Now it was the Joshua generation's turn: the young, the
fearless, the strong. It was their time to make their mark. God
was telling Joshua to honor Moses' ministry, but not copy it.
Every season has a reason.

To execute God's unique plan, Joshua needed strong faith.
So, God gave him special instructions:

"No man shall be able to stand before you all the days
of your life; as I was with Moses, so I will be with you.
I will not leave you nor forsake you. Be strong and of
good courage, for to this people you shall divide as an
inheritance the land which I swore to their fathers to
give them. Only be strong and very courageous, that
you may observe to do according to all the law which

Moses My servant commanded you; do not turn from it to the right hand or to the left, that you may prosper wherever you go. This Book of the Law shall not depart from your mouth, but you shall meditate in it day and night, that you may observe to do according to all that is written in it. For then you will make your way prosperous, and then you will have good success. Have I not commanded you? Be strong and of good courage; do not be afraid, nor be dismayed, for the Lord your God is with you wherever you go." (Joshua 1:5-9)

The Lord repeated himself three times to Joshua to "...be strong and courageous!" Three times! What God told Joshua, he, in turn, told the leaders:

Then Joshua commanded the officers of the people, saying, "Pass through the camp and command the people, saying, 'Prepare provisions for yourselves, for within three days you will cross over this Jordan, to go in to possess the land which the Lord your God is giving you to possess.'" (Joshua 1:11-12)

This daunting task began with a crossing over somewhat similar to the Exodus experience of passing through the Red Sea. Here, it was another body of water, the overflowing river Jordan:

"Now, therefore, take for yourselves twelve men from the tribes of Israel, one man from every tribe. And it shall come to pass, as soon as the soles of the feet of the priests who bear the ark of the Lord, the Lord of all the

earth, shall rest in the waters of the Jordan, that the waters of the Jordan shall be cut off, the waters that come down from upstream, and they shall stand as a heap." So it was, when the people set out from their camp to cross over the Jordan, with the priests bearing the ark of the covenant before the people, and as those who bore the ark came to the Jordan, and the feet of the priests who bore the ark dipped in the edge of the water (for the Jordan overflows all its banks during the whole time of harvest). (Joshua 3:12-15)

And it came to pass, when Joshua was by Jericho, that he lifted his eyes and looked, and behold, a Man stood opposite him with His sword drawn in His hand. And Joshua went to Him and said to Him, "Are You for us or for our adversaries?" So He said, "No, but as Commander of the army of the Lord I have now come." And Joshua fell on his face to the earth and worshiped, and said to Him, "What does my Lord say to His servant?" Then the Commander of the Lord's army said to Joshua, "Take your sandal off your foot, for the place where you stand is holy." And Joshua did so. (Joshua 5:13-15)

Joshua was alone, obviously thinking, praying, and observing his huge task at hand. He was close to his target, Jericho, and all of a sudden Christ shows up. Joshua is the general of Israel's army but the Generalissimo of Generals, Christ, comes on the scene.

Our Blessed Commander had His sword drawn, which

signified a readiness to do warfare. It was a sign to Joshua.

"I am with you and will fight with you and for you, son."

Our General Jesus already has a plan to take our city!

> *"At that time the Lord said to Joshua, "Make flint knives for yourself, and circumcise the sons of Israel again the second time." So Joshua made flint knives for himself, and circumcised the sons of Israel at the hill of the foreskins. And this is the reason why Joshua circumcised them: All the people who came out of Egypt who were males, all the men of war, had died in the wilderness on the way, after they had come out of Egypt. For all the people who came out had been circumcised, but all the people born in the wilderness, on the way as they came out of Egypt, had not been circumcised." (Joshua 6:2-5)*

A strange strategy, but one guaranteed to work; "His ways and his thoughts are not ours…"

Every city is different — It's defenses, strongholds, traditions, and culture begs for a word of wisdom from heaven to give us God's plan so we can impact our cities for Christ.

We see here the two key weapons of warfare to take Jericho are obedience and worship. Of course, without faith none of this would have worked. By faith the walls of Jericho fell down after they were encircled for seven days.

Since 1980 we have registered over 100,000 members at Jubilee. Many of these were new converts to Christ. This represents around ten percent of the total citizens in our city of San Jose.

Has Jubilee impacted the South Bay? Yes, it has. For decades we have had one of the lowest crime rates in America, the highest per-capita income, and we have enjoyed favor with City Hall and City Council, year after year.

We occasionally have challenges, but we're up for the task. My chief calling, at my age, is to ensure the next generation is equipped and prepared to continue the work and continue to take the city:

> And the Lord said to Joshua: "See! I have given Jericho into your hand, it's king, and the mighty men of valor." (Joshua 6:2)

You can do the same thing for your city, or your home.

" The efficiency of strongholds depends on their concealment. Like the underwater mine, once discovered, they can be disarmed."
— *Ed Silvoso*

CHAPTER 32

Making Demons Homeless

Every city or town in America has the homeless. It's a growing problem in large cities like San Francisco. The metrics are staggering. San Francisco is reaching an epidemic problem and nearly every night on the local news there is a story relating to the homeless: deaths, hypothermia, violence, conflict with merchants, and aggressive panhandling.

The solution to homelessness is not simple. The ups and downs of our economy exacerbate the problem, especially during a recession. Here, in the Bay Area, housing is a challenge. The demand for high-paying Silicon Valley jobs has caused our housing market to skyrocket. Finding affordable housing is a big challenge.

Jubilee Christian Center has been involved in helping the homeless in the South Bay for a long while, giving aid, clothing, sleeping bags, and doing as much as we can to alleviate some of the pain of homelessness.

Yes, we want people to have homes. However, when it comes to the demonic community, we love to make them homeless. It's our mission, our calling, and our duty.

A problem I see with the new, cool, modern church is that personal success and happiness seems to be at the forefront of ministry, and power ministry has taken a back seat. Prayer, praying in the Spirit, fasting, using one's authority in Jesus name, laying hands on the sick and casting out demons seems to have been locked up and remembered only in a historical context. Even Pentecostal, neo-Pentecostal, and Charismatic churches, who have a rich history of power ministry, have watered down their message to attract crowds.

Of course, all pastors and ministers want their churches and ministries to grow; but is Jesus interested in crowds, or results?

A man joined our church a while back after spending over twenty years in a local church that had a Pentecostal past. I usually don't interview new members about why they left, but he insisted that I know his decision to leave his church. He went on to tell me it had been years since the blood of Jesus was mentioned, or hell, or healing, or deliverance, and there were no more altar calls. He said very few raised their hands, no one spoke in tongues, and there was no mention of homosexuality, abortion, or Islamic terrorists.

I knew of the church, and I had in year's past called the Pastor a friend. However, this wasn't the first time that I had heard about his church moving away from its Pentecostal roots. It's none of my business how churches operate or present the gospel. All I know is there is a real and present danger if we don't confront the powers of darkness.

I love the book of Ephesians. It's full of wonderful truths and revelation. I love that it sets up three different arenas: Who we are in Christ; where we are in Christ; and what we are in Christ.

Paul wraps that up better with this:

> *Put on the whole armor of God, that you may be able to stand against the wiles of the devil. For we do not wrestle against flesh and blood, but against principalities, against powers, against the rulers of the darkness of this age, against spiritual hosts of wickedness in the heavenly places. Therefore take up the whole armor of God, that you may be able to withstand in the evil day, and having done all, to stand. Stand therefore, having girded your waist with truth, having put on the breastplate of righteousness, and having shod your feet with the preparation of the gospel of peace; above all, taking the shield of faith with which you will be able to quench all the fiery darts of the wicked one. And take the helmet of salvation, and the sword of the Spirit, which is the word of God; praying always with all prayer and supplication in the Spirit, being watchful to this end with all perseverance and supplication for all the saints, and for me, that utterance may be given to me, that I may open my mouth boldly to make known the mystery of the gospel, for which I am an ambassador in chains; that in it I may speak boldly, as I ought to speak. (Ephesians 6:11-20)*

Paul understood spiritual warfare and wrote about it often:

So that you come short in no gift, eagerly waiting for the revelation of our Lord Jesus Christ. (1 Corinthians 1:7)

For though we walk in the flesh, we do not war according to the flesh. For the weapons of our warfare are not carnal but mighty in God for pulling down strongholds, casting down arguments and every high thing that exalts itself against the knowledge of God, bringing every thought into captivity to the obedience of Christ. (2 Corinthians 10:3-5)

This charge I commit to you, son Timothy, according to the prophecies previously made concerning you, that by them you may wage the good warfare. (1 Timothy 1:18)

David said this:

He teaches my hands to make war, So that my arms can bend a bow of bronze. (Psalm 18:34)

Solomon wrote:

Plans are established by counsel; By wise counsel wage war. (Proverbs 20:18)

Even Jesus had something to say on the subject:

Or what king, going to make war against another king, does not sit down first and consider whether he is able with ten thousand to meet him who comes against him with twenty thousand? (Luke 14:31)

Getting back to Paul's exhortation in Ephesians:

Finally, my brethren, be strong in the Lord, and in the power of his might. (Ephesians 6:10)

He begins with "Finally." In other words, after you read and digest all that I wrote in the first five chapters, now, listen up, this is vital, "Be strong in the Lord and in the power of His might."

If life in the natural is an ongoing struggle, how much more is our warfare in the spirit realm? Soldiers, here in American need to be stout-hearted, brave, and well armed to protect our blessed land and to help our friends abroad. How much more do Christian soldiers face as they battle a war both seen and unseen?

Years ago, one little church mother gently rebuked me for teaching so much on warfare and war tactics, conventional and spiritual. I was showing videos, slides, and playing warfare songs to highlight my series. She was offended by it, and she wanted more teaching on love, mercy, grace, and the fruit of the spirit.

I agree that those virtues are extremely important, but so is this topic. As C.S. Lewis said, "To be overly enamored with the demonic is foolish, but to ignore them is dangerous." One friend put it this way, "If a baby's diaper is dirty, it needs to be changed, and the quicker the better, or it stinks up everything."

Again, Paul makes sure our resolve and our strength is in Jesus, in His cause, in His might, and for His sake! He tells us to "Put on the whole armor of God." Remember, give Satan an inch and he'll try to take a mile. Leave a little opening in the door and he'll attempt to kick it wide open. His art, experience, and trafficking is formidable.

The enemy's team is ranked by position and power: Principalities (rulers), powers (or authorities), cosmic power (or dark forces), and wicked spirits in high places (or unclean spirits). Paul reminds us the devil has strategies, wiles, tricks, that he's perfected over millenniums to destroy man.

Never forget, Satan is a prince. He's the prince of darkness! Paul also called him "The prince of the power of the air (atmosphere)."

We also know that many of the fallen angels are kept chained in Tartarus, the lowest rejoins of Hades (hell).

> *For if God spared not the angels that sinned, but cast them down to hell, and delivered them into chains of darkness, to be reserved unto judgment. (2 Peter 2:4)*

Here's another supporting scripture:

> *And the angels who did not keep their proper domain, but left their own abode, He has reserved in everlasting chains under darkness for the judgment of the great day. (Jude 1:6)*

There's no small debate as to why some fallen Angels are imprisoned and others free to roam the atmosphere and the earth under Satan's command. Some suggest there were two waves of fallen angels.

Here is the first wave:

In the beginning God created the heavens and the earth. The earth was without form, and void; and darkness was on the face of the deep. And the Spirit of God was hovering over the face of the waters. (Genesis 1:1-2)

We know something chaotic happened just by looking at the language of verse 2. Some called this the first flawed, or the pre-antediluvian period. Some call it *Lucifer's flood*, or the *gap theory*.

Was Lucifer's domain earth way before our parents, Adam and Eve, came on the scene? No one knows, but it's interesting to speculate.

Look at it again:

The earth was without form, and void; and darkness was on the face of the deep. And the Spirit of God was hovering over the face of the waters. (Genesis 1:1)

It says; "The earth was without form," or *tohus*, in Hebrew, which means a *waste place, desolate worthless, a descent or wilderness*. The verse goes on to add "and void," or *bohuw*, which translates *empty, ruined, a vacuum!* Whoa, Nelly! It gets worse: "And darkness was on the face of the deep" *Darkness?* The Hebrew word here is *choshek* (pronounced Khoshek), which means *misery, confusion, sorrow, ignorance, and destruction.*

God did not create the world just to let it go to hell. Something catastrophic happened. Was there a second wave of rebellion launched from earth? Is this what Isaiah, chapter 14, is referring to? Could it be these Angels who followed Lucifer are today free to roam, and not locked up like the first rebellion? I don't know, but this I do know. Demons are real and we must, as a *Body of Believers,* take care of our Father's business.

Paul had more to say about this:

To me, who am less than the least of all the saints, this grace was given, that I should preach among the Gentiles the unsearchable riches of Christ, and to make all see what is the fellowship of the mystery, which from the beginning of the ages has been hidden in God who created all things through Jesus Christ; to the intent that now the manifold wisdom of God might be made known by the church to the principalities and powers in the heavenly places, according to the eternal purpose which He accomplished in Christ Jesus our Lord, in whom we have boldness and access with confidence through faith in Him. (Ephesians 3:8-12)

First, this mystery of redemption and salvation for all, Jew and Gentile, which God kept as a secret from the beginning, but now, because of Christ, is revealed. And secondly, this great revelation not only is exposed to all men but also must be proclaimed to the principalities and powers in the heavenlies through or by the church! Amazing!

The hosts of heaven are organized by rank and file. Satan copied God's organizational chart and assigned his evil minions according to ability.

I'm sure if a fallen angel were high ranking he would be a prince or principality. It appears Paul is letting us know God's good angels are willing and able to assist us in ministry, and the fallen foes need to be told just how it is — we have authority over them, through the church, in Jesus' name!

Looking again at the armor of God, notice it's His armor, not ours. It's designed to help us hold our ground and to advance. "Having done all to stand, stand therefore..."

Most of the armor is defensive, a shield, a helmet, a belt, a breastplate — even one's feet are protected.

Paul says, "Truth, righteousness, peace, faith, and salvation" are precious things that need daily protection, because Satan never quits. However, the one offensive weapon is the sword, which is the word of God.

Satan has no defense for the Word when it is read, listened to, shared, taught, preached, and memorized. Stubborn, carnal, Dick Bernal had no defense for it, the Word, back in 1977. However, once I actually listened to it, as shared by my wife, Carla, and preached by a local Pastor, it stabbed me in my heart!

For the word of God is living and powerful, and sharper than any two-edged sword, piercing even to the division of soul and spirit, and of joints and marrow, and is a discerner of the thoughts and intents of the heart. And there is no creature hidden from His sight, but all things are naked and open to the eyes of Him to whom we must give account. (Hebrews 4:12-13)

I like serving demons an eviction notice! Not thirty or forty-five days grace period. Immediate eviction!

"When an unclean spirit goes out of a man, he goes through dry places, seeking rest, and finds none. Then he says, 'I will return to my house from which I came.' And when he comes, he finds it empty, swept, and put in order. Then he goes and takes with him seven other spirits more wicked than himself, and they enter and dwell there; and the last state of that man is worse than the first. So shall it also be with this wicked generation." (Matthew 12:43-45)

Then they brought him to Him. And when he saw Him, immediately the spirit convulsed him, and he fell on the ground and wallowed, foaming at the mouth. So He asked his father, "How long has this been happening to him?" And he said, "From childhood. And often he has thrown him both into the fire and into the water to destroy him. But if You can do anything, have compassion on us and help us." (Mark 9:21-22)

Jesus said to him, "If you can believe, all things are possible to him who believes." Immediately the father of the child cried out and said with tears, "Lord, I believe; help my unbelief!" When Jesus saw that the people came running together, He rebuked the unclean spirit, saying to it: "Deaf and dumb spirit, I command you, come out of him and enter him no more!" Then the spirit cried out, convulsed him greatly, and came out of him. And he became as one dead, so that many said, "He is dead." But Jesus took him by the hand and lifted him up, and he arose. (Mark 9:23-27)

Demons need bodies to exercise their master's will. Kill, steal or destroy! Unclean, or impure spirits — spirits of sickness, disease, or other maladies — need earthly houses. If pressed, they will settle for pigs, as in Mark 5.

I've experienced cases of possession, or at the very least, depression, even obsession. Through openings of doors left unlocked, you could, too. Why do we lock our houses or our cars when we leave? So people can't break in and rob us, or worse.

So how does a demon or do demons gain entry in a human house? In India, it's often because of idol worship. Here in California, in many cases, it's because of drugs or witchcraft. In one case, a friend's son went to a demonic horror movie, and the effects of watching that movie has changed him to this day.

Demons prey on abuse, fear, mental illness, or any situation that will give them a foothold. One man I know got curious about porn on the internet and he got bound with that addiction. He nearly lost everything. It wasn't easy for him to get free, but by God's grace he did. He said he could actually feel spirits of lust moving around in him.

Carla and I once dealt with a teenage girl who played around with a Ouija board doing a séance with her friends. Dangerous! She went through a four-hour exorcism that got ugly, but Jesus won, as always!

You might ask how did the vile spirit finally come out? We kept praying and saying, "In the name of Jesus, you must come out, and the blood of Jesus is against you, you have no power, quit whining, come out now." It was stubborn, but it submitted.

Once in India, a certain poor girl went into a trance. Her eyes rolled back, and I was afraid she was having a seizure, but we pressed on. When the unclean thing came out, it made a tearing sound, like ripping a newspaper or paper bag. I guess it left in a hurry. She came to and was so happy to be free.

Let's keep demons dry!

> *"When an unclean spirit goes out of a man, he goes through dry places, seeking rest; and finding none, he says, 'I will return to my house from which I came.' And when he comes, he finds it swept and put in order. Then he goes and takes with him seven other spirits more wicked than himself, and they enter and dwell there; and the last state of that man is worse than the first."* (Luke 11:24-26)

As Christian's we have authority over darkness, devils, and demons! We have all the weapons to destroy the enemy's plans for our lives, and a King who goes before us and has already equipped us for battle. We must not take Satan's attacks lying down or simply trump them up to God's will or think that's just the way it goes. We are soldiers who need to fight back the kingdom of darkness and take everything back everything that has been stolen from us.

Let's increase the demonic homeless statistics a hundredfold starting today!

" Faith is dead to doubts, dumb to discouragement, blind to impossibilities, and knows nothing but success."

— *Wayne Meyers*

" Ignore criticism…
Ever see a barking dog
stop a speeding train?
Stay on track, don't
slow down."
— *Oral Roberts*

CHAPTER 33

The Word Works

The local newspaper did a three-page spread about Jubilee and me, years ago. The writer referred to me as a literalist. I wasn't sure if I should be flattered or offended. Jubilee was exploding, and the local paper got wind of it and sniffed me out for a very long interview.

I guess I came across as a literalist — one who literally believes the Bible as actual facts; historical fact, spiritual fact, and future fact. I plead guilty!

A neighbor of mine popped over for coffee and began sharing with me his religious upbringing — some old-line denomination out of the Midwest. He, without hesitation, began telling me how, as a kid, he bought into the whole thing: Noah's ark, Jonah's fish, David and Goliath, the virgin birth, and the incredible story of Christ being raised from the dead. However, as he grew older and began thinking for himself, and with four years of college to lean on, he made up his mind and he said, "The Bible is great. Just don't take it seriously or literally".

I smiled at him and began sharing my faith, and my testimony, and the miracles I've seen. I told him, "Well, as for me, I have no problem believing the Bible, word for word." He didn't argue. He actually admired my resolve.

We became friends, played golf, went to Hawaii, together, with a few other couples. He and his wife joined our church, and I think he began seeing the Bible differently. Eventually, they moved on to another city. I hope they're doing well.

Paul makes my point for me:

> For though we walk in the flesh, we do not war according to the flesh. For the weapons of our warfare are not carnal but mighty in God for pulling down strongholds, casting down arguments and every high thing that exalts itself against the knowledge of God, bringing every thought into captivity to the obedience of Christ, and being ready to punish all disobedience when your obedience is fulfilled. (2 Corinthians 10:3-6)

Spiritual warfare is, according to Paul, a battle that cannot be waged in the flesh. Believe me, demons know the difference. Do you remember the Sons of Sceva? The demons said, "Jesus we know, Paul we know, who are you?"

Let me break this down for you: These preachers' kids (sons of a priest) thought, because our dad serves God, we've got the goods. Bad idea! They nearly got themselves killed in the process.

My first missionary trip to India proved this to be true. I was simply tagging along with a veteran Pastor, Larry Huggins, to a third world nation that has a culture of idolatry and superstition.

I thought I would be an observer not a participant. However, things changed rapidly. I was thrust into the role of preacher, evangelist, healer, and deliverer of demonic forces. I had to get into the Spirit fast and furiously.

Prayer and fasting really does expedite the process. My training in the word, and my understanding of the authority of the believer, and my knowledge of the armor of God and the power of God got me through a tough week in Guntor, India.

By the third night, I was actually looking forward to setting the possessed free, because we had such wonderful results the first two nights.

Back to our text in 2 Corinthians, Paul speaks of weaponry. Our tools of eviction are not conventional or carnal, but they are mighty and very powerful for the pulling down of strongholds.

I've noticed something these last thirty-six-plus years of traveling this planet. The most successful ministries – the large, city-impacting ministries that attract huge crowds and have worldwide reputations — seem to have a common thread. The leaders are all humble, meek, and surprised at their own success. They are kind, generous, and they have a healthy sense of humor.

I've been privileged to be friends with many of these successful ministers, and I've learned a few things from them. I've learned to lead by love, walk by faith, live with mercy and grace, and to do those things daily.

Satan's character is proud, boastful, arrogant, hateful, violent, a liar, conniver, and a trickster. We should fight to be the exact opposite:

Then Jesus was led up by the Spirit into the wilderness to be tempted by the devil. (Matthew 4:1)

Knowing a frontal assault was coming, Jesus fasted and prayed for forty long days and nights. Satan, who waits for a sign of weakness — as a lion stalks a herd of wilderbeasts - waits for starvation to set in, then approaches.

Like Eve in the garden, Satan brings into question the validity of God's word, and our stand upon on it.

ROUND ONE

Now when the tempter came to Him, he said, "If You are the Son of God, command that these stones become bread." (Matthew 4:3)

Jesus reaches into his scabbard and pulls out his sword: "It is written!" He simply quotes God's word as the antidote to the temptation.

Is he hungry? Absolutely! He was beyond hungry. Does bread sound good? It's like you can hear the tempter saying, "C'mon, Jesus can't you smell fresh bread? Hey, you deserve a loaf. Go for it!" (Interestingly, Eve's temptation was also the appeal of food – the forbidden fruit).

Let me parenthetically add, fasting doesn't make us spiritually strong; it actually makes us weak and dependent on God for our strength. It's humbling to realize how much we crave food, and what a big part of our lives it plays.

Ouch! The sword hurt! Ah! The Old Serpent was taken back. He was wounded, but he wasn't ready to give up. So, he used a different tactic.

ROUND TWO

Like boxers who are losing, Satan switches his style. He took Jesus to Jerusalem and the temple. The wilderness, probably the Sinai desert, was void of people, but there were huge crowds at the temple. "Listen, Jesus, let me be your P.R. guy. Throw yourself off this pinnacle, yell real loud, all will look up and see you falling, and when the angels catch you... BOOM! Instant fame! You're a celebrity and everyone knows it. Your welcome Jesus – glad to help!"

> "If You are the Son of God, throw Yourself down. For it is written: 'He shall give His angels charge over you,' and, 'In their hands they shall bear you up, lest you dash your foot against a stone.'" (Matthew 4:6)

Jesus uses the sword of the Spirit again:

> "It is written again, 'You shall not tempt the Lord your God.'" (Matthew 4:5-7)

This is spiritual warfare at it's highest — the Prince of Peace versus the Prince of Darkness.

Unlike great sporting events today with millions watching, this was one-on-one, with no human eyes watching. However, I think heaven's host, hell's demons, and God himself were ringside.

Satan had to be getting discouraged. He gave Jesus two solid shots but our Lord still stood strong even though He was starving, lonely, and tired.

ROUND THREE

Then, here comes, as they say, the kitchen sink. Satan had one final go at it. It was his best shot, his big push:

> *Again, the devil took Him up on an exceedingly high mountain, and showed Him all the kingdoms of the world and their glory. And he said to Him, "All these things I will give You if You will fall down and worship me." Then Jesus said to him, "Away with you, Satan! For it is written, 'You shall worship the Lord your God, and Him only you shall serve.'" Then the devil left Him, and behold, angels came and ministered to Him. (Matthew 4:8-11)*

Unlike God, Satan saves the worst for last! He takes him to a high mountain or high place. Some suggest it was mount Pisgah in Jordan where God told Moses to go:

> *"Go up to the top of Pisgah, and lift your eyes toward the west, the north, the south, and the east; behold it with your eyes, for you shall not cross over this Jordan. But command Joshua, and encourage him and strengthen him; for he shall go over before this people, and he shall cause them to inherit the land which you will see." (Deuteronomy 3:27-28)*

Satan's ego is exposed in the wilderness experience. He acts like he owns everything and can keep it or give it at a whim. Obviously, Satan is not all knowing, but some knowing, and aware of Christ's mission to turn all the kingdoms of the earth into the kingdoms of God:

Then the seventh angel sounded: And there were loud voices in heaven, saying, "The kingdoms of this world have become the kingdoms of our Lord and of His Christ, and He shall reign forever and ever!" (Revelation 11:15)

Before the wilderness experience, John the Baptist baptized Jesus in the river Jordan. From there, Jesus would see things and places he'd never seen before. Also, it's why I believe our Lord was in Jordan:

John answered them, saying, "I baptize with water, but there stands One among you whom you do not know. It is He who, coming after me, is preferred before me, whose sandal strap I am not worthy to loose." These things were done in Bethabara beyond the Jordan, where John was baptizing. The next day John saw Jesus coming toward him, and said, "Behold! The Lamb of God who takes away the sin of the world!" (John 1:26-29)

Satan, the author behind all idolatry and pagan worship, who received and craved it, tried to seduce our Lord into what the world had become — a world deceived into believing idols made with hands were gods.

Jesus finally had enough! I'm sure even weak, weary, and starving, he shouted, "Away with you! Hit the road jack! Split! Burn rubber, "For it is written…""

Why change tactics even though one is angry, fed up, and sick of ongoing temptation. Keep swinging the sword. Jesus again reaches into his scabbard and pulls out:

"You shall fear the Lord your God and serve Him, and shall take oaths in His name." (Deuteronomy 6:13)

This had to absolutely baffle and confuse Satan. His best bait wasn't enough to get Jesus to bite, as Eve and Adam did:

And I will put enmity between you and the woman, and between your seed and her Seed; He shall bruise your head, and you shall bruise His heel. (Genesis 3:15)

This scripture had truly come alive while Jesus was in the desert.

Jesus, the seed of Mary, a seed from heaven had crushed the serpent's head. With his tail between his legs, Satan limped off to try and figure out another strategy.

I love the part where the angels then came and ministered to our Lord. The spirit world was watching like fans of opposing teams, both sides cheering for their heroes. In this case, Jesus' side had to be ecstatic: "Jesus three — Satan zero." A shutout!

No matter where you are, how you're feeling, what's going on in you or around you, the Word of God in your heart and mind, and coming out of your mouth in faith, works! The word works!

Then the Lord put forth His hand and touched my mouth, and the Lord said to me: "Behold, I have put My words in your mouth. See, I have this day set you over the nations and over the kingdoms, to root out and to pull down, To destroy and to throw down, To build and to plant." (Jeremiah 1:9-10)

CHAPTER 34

Toto, This Ain't Kansas

Over 400 years, ago my Spanish forefathers boarded a ship somewhere in Spain, and headed for Mexico, in the New World. After some exploring, they headed up north to what now is California. The King of Spain gave those early pioneers land grants.

Monterey, California was the first capital, then my city, San Jose, and eventually, Sacramento (named after the sacraments). California was explored and settled in the name of God and King. In 1850, when California was made a state, the legislature met in San Jose to make it official.

The Catholic Church's influence can be seen up and down the state. Cities are named after Saints, angels, and the famous missionary, Father Junipero Serra, who built missions from San Diego to San Francisco over a span of thirteen years. In all, twenty-one missions were built to spread Catholicism throughout California. This hard working Franciscan Friar died at the age of seventy and is buried at his beloved Mission Carmel.

The discovery of gold in the Sacramento Valley in early 1848 sparked a gold rush. One of the great events to help shape American history and exposed the west to all the world. The Forty-Niners flocked to California seeking fortune and fame.

Before 1848, the non-native population was under 1,000. By 1849, a year before California was granted statehood, over 100,000 settlers were living in this new land.

Today, as of this writing, California has nearly 40 million residents and an economy that rivals nations. I happen to live and pastor in the heart of Silicon Valley. The high-tech boom happened on my watch. We started Jubilee in November 1980. A brand new fledgling company called Apple was in its infancy. Within a relatively short period of time, our Valley, known more for fruit production, would be ground zero for technological innovation.

When guests come from around the U.S. or abroad, I usually give them choices for sightseeing. I often suggest San Francisco or Carmel-Monterey. Both within an hour drive! More often than not, they'll say, "Can we visit Apple, Facebook, Google, or some other hot local company?"

Yes, times have changed.

What about the Gospel, evangelism, city transformation, or a good old fashioned revival in this area? The Bay Area, with nearly eight million people is, and has been, hard ground for the gospel of Jesus Christ. The Bay Area is the least church-going metropolitan area in America, and has been for quite a while.

This is not the Bible belt. It's more like the cuff of the trousers. Am I discouraged? No way! For nearly four decades I've looked at my turf as a great mission field. We are the microcosm of the world. Every area, city, and nation has its challenges when it comes to preaching Christ, saving souls, planting churches, establishing marketplace ministries, and ongoing discipleship.

Every region is unique, so we need a strategy. It starts with prayer and ends with praise. America has had to rethink warfare since the Revolutionary conflict. From the Minute Men Militia, to the Civil War, WWI, WWII, Korea, Vietnam, and now the ongoing battle to protect America from terrorism. It's not business as usual.

I would suggest spiritual warfare is the same. We, the church, are not a sub-culture but a counter culture.

The devil and his cadre are not passive. They are never going to give us a break. They never have and they never will. We cannot be like the Jews, who from Nebuchadnezzar to Adolf Hitler, thought, "Just ignore evil and evil will ignore you." Never! Satan has an agenda that we must not ignore.

He doesn't need a hug, or need to be understood, or as the Rolling Stones sang, sympathized with. He needs to be defeated on all fronts.

Jesus showed us the way, and Paul added warfare tactics that work. John also had this advice:

Little children, let no one deceive you. He who practices righteousness is righteous, just as He is righteous. He who sins is of the devil, for the devil has sinned from the beginning. For this purpose the Son of God was manifested, that He might destroy the works of the devil. (1 John 3:7-8)

Jesus made it plain:

"The thief does not come except to steal, and to kill, and to destroy. I have come that they may have life, and that they may have it more abundantly." (John 10:10)

Jesus wants us to have an abundant, blessed, wonderful, fruitful, productive life. But we have to fight for it.

This book, with prayer, will help you to win on every front.

" Champions are a rare breed. They see beyond the dangers, the risks, the obstacles, and the hardships"

— Lester Sumrall

CHAPTER 35

Got to Get Back to the Garden – Crosby, Stills, Nash & Young

From the late sixties through the middle seventies folk, rock and hard rock were a big part of my social life. Living close to the city of San Francisco, my buddies and I would frequent the San Francisco scene on Friday nights, usually at the iconic Fillmore Auditorium. The hottest groups or solo artist would be there on any given Friday.

Not being saved or living for Christ at that time allowed my flesh to tune in, turn on, and get lost for a weekend, at least.

Katy Perry's dad, Keith Hudson (Katy took her mother's maiden name Perry so she wouldn't be confused with actress Kate Hudson) can relate to my past. For a season, Keith was a disciple of Timothy Leary, the godfather of the psychedelic movement. Keith shared his stories with me about that era. Both of us shake our heads in disbelief that we survived. Oh, but for the grace of God! Looking back, and on occasion, listening to some of the old classics that earmarked that zeitgeist, I'm amazed how many songs had bible references or some spiritual connotation.

In 1965, the Byrds sang the old Pete Seeger song, *Turn, Turn, Turn*. The words were taken right out of the third chapter of Ecclesiastes.

My favorite folk-rock group was Crosby, Stills & Nash, and on occasion Neil Young. I would sing along with them, "Got to get back to the garden," not realizing they were referring to Eden. A lot of young people were searching back in those days for spiritual relevance and hope. That didn't happen for me until 1977.

Some call the Garden of Eden, a piece of heaven on earth, paradise. Eden means *delight and pleasure*. It was a place of happiness and holiness. No houses were needed, nor clothes, nor any of the trappings of the modern world for that matter. There were no churches, or bibles, or even preachers because man was perfect. He could daily visit with God. Perhaps he could even see angels, as it was heaven on a piece of earth.

One will never fully understand spiritual warfare without closely looking at Satan's first assault on humanity. Lucifer, an angel of light — perhaps the highest ranking of these beautiful celestial spirits — rebelled against God, and somehow convinced a large group of his species to follow in his doomed mission to dethrone God:

> *How you are fallen from heaven, O Lucifer, son of the morning! How you are cut down to the ground, You who weakened the nations! For you have said in your heart: 'I will ascend into heaven, I will exalt my throne above the stars of God; I will also sit on the mount of the congregation On the farthest sides of the north;*

I will ascend above the heights of the clouds, I will be like the Most High.' Yet you shall be brought down to Sheol, To the lowest depths of the Pit. "Those who see you will gaze at you, And consider you, saying, 'Is this the man who made the earth tremble, Who shook kingdoms, Who made the world as a wilderness and destroyed its cities, Who did not open the house of his prisoners?' All the kings of the nations, All of them, sleep in glory, Everyone in his own house; But you are cast out of your grave Like an abominable branch, like the garment of those who are slain, Thrust through with a sword, who go down to the stones of the pit, Like a corpse trodden underfoot." (Isaiah 14:12-19)

Here, in the narrative, Isaiah is targeting the literal King of Babylon. However many bible scholars believe it holds two-fold truth:

It shall come to pass in the day the Lord gives you rest from your sorrow, and from your fear and the hard bondage in which you were made to serve, that you will take up this proverb against the king of Babylon, and say: "How the oppressor has ceased, The golden city ceased! The Lord has broken the staff of the wicked, the scepter of the rulers; He who struck the people in wrath with a continual stroke, he who ruled the nations in anger, is persecuted and no one hinders. The whole earth is at rest and quiet; They break forth into singing. Indeed the cypress trees rejoice over you, and the cedars of Lebanon, Saying, 'Since you were cut down, No woodsman has come up against us.' Hell from beneath

is excited about you, To meet you at your coming;
It stirs up the dead for you, All the chief ones of the
earth; It has raised up from their thrones All the kings
of the nations." (Isaiah 14:3-9)

Babylon, the very name means to *overflow, mingle, mix and*
confuse. From Nimrod to Nebuchadnezzar, between and
beyond, kings of Babylon stood stiff and strong against God
and His people. The spirit behind this evil dynasty is none
other then Satan himself.

Isaiah's prophecy in chapter fourteen has a two-fold aim.
Even if the prophet wasn't aware, he was also prophesying
and predicting Satan's ultimate demise.

Through the Bible, Old and New Testament Babylon is
synonymous with the world's agenda.

Let's go back to the garden:

Now the serpent was more cunning than any beast of
the field which the Lord God had made. And he said
to the woman, "Has God indeed said, 'You shall not
eat of every tree of the garden?'" And the woman said
to the serpent, "We may eat the fruit of the trees of the
garden; but of the fruit of the tree which is in the midst
of the garden, God has said, 'You shall not eat it, nor
shall you touch it, lest you die.'" Then the serpent said
to the woman, "You will not surely die." (Genesis 3:1-4)

This assault on our first parents gives us clues to the wiles of
the devil.

The devil's disguise is interesting — a serpent! Most of us

are not too fond of snakes. Recently, I was taking out the garbage. I didn't know it, but a four-foot gopher snake had slithered into the container. A gopher snake looks similar to rattlesnakes where I live. At first glance, I nearly jumped onto the hood of my GMC, "whoa Nelly!" Once I realized it was a harmless creature, even though I still didn't like its appearance, I grabbed a broom and shooed it out.

I don't think Satan meant to scare Eve into sin, but to tempt her. We are tempted with things that attract the flesh, not by things that repel it. Some bible scholars believe the serpent of the garden walked upright or may have been a flying serpent descending from above, imitating an angel. Whatever its appearance may have been, it got Eve's attention enough to engage her in dialogue.

Satan's agenda is to get us away from God and each other — to conqueror and divide. He waits patiently as a snake does, for its dinner. Once Eve was somewhat separated from Adam, the devil went to work. Adam got the command, first hand from God not to partake of the forbidden fruit:

Then the Lord God took the man and put him in the garden of Eden to tend and keep it. And the Lord God commanded the man, saying, "Of every tree of the garden you may freely eat; but of the tree of the knowledge of good and evil you shall not eat, for in the day that you eat of it you shall surely die." (Genesis 2:15-17)

Eve was not made as of yet, so it would have been her husband's responsibility to share with her God's orders. It could have been Eve was looking at the tree of the knowledge of good and evil with curiosity, which allowed Satan to make his move.

Satan brings into question what sin is, much like today. "Has God indeed said you can't? Did God tell you? Who told you? Are you for sure? Eve, my dear, is that fair?"

> *Now the serpent was more cunning than any beast of the field which the Lord God had made. And he said to the woman, "Has God indeed said, 'You shall not eat of every tree of the garden?'" (Genesis 3:1)*

He quotes the command fallaciously, "Has God indeed said you shall not eat of every tree of the garden?"

Twisting God's word is always the first tactic of the enemy. The word of God can't be reproached until first it's misrepresented. To draw people into sin, Satan puts a spin on God's Word as unreasonable. Eve's first mistake was she engaged in conversation with him instead of calling her husband over, or simply rebuking the devil and commanding him to leave.

One old sage wrote, "To stay out of harm, stay out of harm's way."

Did her curiosity get to her? *Wow! A talking serpent! It's beautiful to look at. It seems like a caring, interesting sort of creature. Perhaps it's a future friend?*

Her answer is, for the most part, spot on. "We may eat the fruit of the trees of the garden, but that which is in the midst of the garden, God has said you shall not eat it, nor shall you touch it, least you die."

Ok, she's close but God said nothing about not touching it. She added that part. Adding to the Word is as bad as taking away from God's word.

Here's an ongoing problem with religion – adding to what God said. Man, sometimes, even with good intentions, adds his own ideas of what is right or wrong.

For example, abstinence has its place in the Christian conscience, but some read it this way: *If abstaining from one tree pleases God, how about ten trees or twenty trees?* Soon, this brand of religion sucks all the color out of life:

> *Then the serpent said to the woman, "You will not surely die." (Genesis 3:4)*

Here, in verse 4, Satan gets a little bolder by contradicting what God said. If he can get us to doubt, he then can get us to deny!

Again, Satan uses a half-truth to poison a virtuous mind. God didn't mean if you eat the fruit, you immediately drop dead — physically gone, buried. No, he was referring to an immediate spiritual death and an eventual physical death, which wouldn't have happened if Adam and Eve had not fallen.

First doubt, then deny, then you'll discover a bigger world of salacious information. Eve, God hasn't been fair with you...

> *For God knows that in the day you eat of it your eyes will be opened, and you will be like God, knowing good and evil. (Genesis 3:5)*

Sin always promises a brighter future, a happier life, more fun, excitement, and adventure. It taunts you to look how green the grass is on the other side of the pasture.

"Listen Eve, God, for some selfish reason, is holding you back from being like Him. Open your eyes, girl. Eat, be free, live the life you deserve."

This wasn't Satan's first rodeo. His deceptive ways worked on one third of the angels in heaven, "Follow me and I will make you all better!"

It was too much for Eve. She bit! She bit because the serpent bit her, venom clouded her mind, and now we have the beginning of fallen humanity.

One of the great perplexities of all of the holy writ is why did Adam join in? Much has been written, surmised, even preached about this passage:

> So when the woman saw that the tree was good for food, that it was pleasant to the eyes, and a tree desirable to make one wise, she took of its fruit and ate. She also gave to her husband with her, and he ate. Then the eyes of both of them were opened, and they knew that they were naked; and they sewed fig leaves together and made themselves coverings. And they heard the sound of the Lord God walking in the garden in the cool of the day, and Adam and his wife hid themselves from the presence of the Lord God among the trees of the garden. Then the Lord God called to Adam and said to him, "Where are you?" So he said, "I heard Your voice in the garden, and I was afraid because I was naked; and I hid myself." And He said, "Who told you that you were naked? Have you eaten from the tree of which I

commanded you that you should not eat?" Then the man said, "The woman whom You gave to be with me, she gave me of the tree, and I ate." (Genesis 3:6-12)

Did Eve share word for word with Adam what she heard? Did she say, "Look, I'm alive, I didn't drop dead." Perhaps she said, "Boy, Adam, this is delicious. Here, try it, it's good."

Or was his love for her so strong he couldn't imagine being separated from her? No one knows for sure, but it happened. Soon after, fear, guilt, shame flooded their minds and emotions, and they were fallen, sinful creatures hiding from God.

Notice, they didn't flee the garden. They stayed there.

They tried to hide like sinners who attend church, knowing full well that they're not right with God. They may be hungry for His presence and His Word, but they're hiding on the back pew, hoping that by some kind of mysterious osmosis they can get a little righteousness sprinkled on them.

God never asks a question He doesn't know the answer to. God knew exactly what tree or bush they were hiding behind. He was asking, "Where are you?" He was trying to get Adam and Eve to think, "Yeah, where in the heck are we?"

Once Adam and Eve realized they were naked, they created the world's first false religion – the fig leaf religion. They tried to cover their shame and nakedness with fig leaves.

The word atone means to cover. Were our parents trying to atone for their transgression? The biggest problem here is fig leaves have no blood in them. It's a false atonement. Likewise, good works and good deeds are like fig leaves. They won't get people into heaven.

"Without the shedding of blood there is no remission of sin." I wrote a book, *Shaking Hands with God,* on this very subject, also known as Blood Covenant.

Was God upset with what happened to Adam and Eve? Sure He was. Was He done with Adam and Eve? No!

> *Also for Adam and his wife the Lord God made tunics of skin, and clothed them. Then the Lord God said, "Behold, the man has become like one of Us, to know good and evil. And now, lest he put out his hand and take also of the tree of life, and eat, and live forever" Therefore the Lord God sent him out of the garden of Eden to till the ground from which he was taken. So He drove out the man; and He placed cherubim at the east of the garden of Eden, and a flaming sword which turned every way, to guard the way to the tree of life. (Genesis 3:21-24)*

Animals, arguably lambs, were slain and innocent blood was shed to cover guilty humanity. Though Adam and Eve were pardoned, it would be a hard road ahead. The good news is, "His mercy endures for ever."

One Sunday morning at church, I grabbed my Bible by the pages. I held up chapters one and two of Genesis, which was page 1 and 2. Then I dangled the rest of the Bible. "God is trying to get us back to the garden."

When I hear that old song by Crosby, Stills, Nash & Young, I smile.

CHAPTER 36

Warfare, Gates, The Pensacola Revival

The Brownsville revival in Pensacola, Florida, began on Father's Day, June 18, 1995, at the Brownsville Assembly of God Church. It was an amazing outpouring of repentance, a call to holiness, and manifestations of the Holy Spirit. It is reported to have attracted over 4 million people from 1995 to 2000.

It was December 23, 1996, when my secretary stopped me as I was leaving the office for our annual Christmas break.

"Pastor, there is a John Kilpatrick on the phone for you."

Being way behind with my Christmas shopping, I hesitated. I was trying to remember this Pastor, and I was tempted to say, "Take his number, and I'll call him later." But I thought what's a few minutes to talk to a fellow Pastor and, besides, it's Christmas.

I picked up the phone.

He said, "Hello, Dick. This is John Kilpatrick."

Not recognizing the name, I simply replied, "Hi John. What can I do for you?"

"Well Dick, I Pastor the Brownsville Assembly of God Church here in Florida. Perhaps you've heard of us?"

"Gee, Pastor, not sure I have. Sorry!"

"Well, have you heard of the Pensacola Revival?"

"Oh sure. Who hasn't?"

"Dick, that's us."

Feeling a bit embarrassed, I said, "Oh, Lord, John, I'm so sorry. Forgive me. What can I do for you?"

"Dick, I wanted to tell you how your book, *Storming Hells Brazen Gates*, helped launch this outpouring. I'm writing a book and, with your permission, I would like to quote several passages from your book."

He went on to say how he preached several Sunday night services using my little warfare book.

For years he had been praying for a revival. Once he brought in evangelist, Steve Hill, it was on!

I sat in my office somewhat stunned and humbled. "Of course, John, quote the whole thing if you want, and, thanks for telling me."

What a Christmas present! Before Pastor John hung up, he encouraged me to come and see what I had a small part in starting. I eventually took around two-hundred folks from our church to witness this amazing open heaven revival over Pensacola, Florida.

Later, I asked the Lord, "Father, I wrote the book, but why did they get the revival 3,000 miles away?"

He didn't answer, but I still got it. John's church cried out for years for a genuine visitation and outpouring of heaven's blessing. Hungry people get heaven's manna.

Remember, Jesus said, "You can have what you ask for if you believe and doubt not in your heart."

My old friend, neighbor, and former teacher from our Bible School, Dr. Ed Murphy, wrote a fantastic book called, *The Handbook for Spiritual Warfare*. He begins his book with an overview, or as he calls it, "The spiritual warfare dimension of a biblical worldview."

Let me quote Dr. Murphy here:

"The biblical worldview dimension can be expressed in one statement: present reality exists in a state of cosmic-earthly conflict, or spiritual warfare. In philosophical terms, modified dualism exists in the universe. The Kingdom of God and the kingdom of evil supernaturalism are engaged in fierce conflict one against the other. Absolute dualism affirms that ultimate reality is eternally dualistic, that evil and good have always existed."

Of course, when there was only God, there was nothing but good, but once He created angels, who had a free will, the chance for evil was there and we now know evil took root in Lucifer and spread to a third of the hosts.

As born again, spirit beings we live in two worlds at the same time. There is conflict and struggle in both realms. When Paul, in Ephesians chapter 6, expounded on this, he reminded us our warfare is not against flesh and blood, but against principalities, powers, rulers of the darkness of this present age and wicked, unclean spirits in heavenly places. Problem is, so many of us get entangled in the horizontal conflict with people, we lose sight of the vertical and the invisible forces.

Jesus to Peter:

> *"And I also say to you that you are Peter, and on this rock, I will build My church, and the gates of Hades shall not prevail against it. And I will give you the keys of the kingdom of heaven, and whatever you bind on earth will be bound in heaven, and whatever you loose on earth will be loosed in heaven. Then He commanded His disciples that they should tell no one that He was Jesus the Christ. From that time Jesus began to show to His disciples that He must go to Jerusalem, and suffer many things from the elders and chief priests and scribes, and be killed, and be raised the third day. Then Peter took Him aside and began to rebuke Him, saying, "Far be it from You, Lord; this shall not happen to You!" But He turned and said to Peter, "Get behind Me, Satan! You are an offense to Me, for you are not*

*mindful of the things of God, but the things of men."
Then Jesus said to His disciples, "If anyone desires to
come after Me, let him deny himself, and take up his
cross, and follow Me. For whoever desires to save his
life will lose it, but whoever loses his life for My sake
will find it. For what profit is it to a man if he gains the
whole world, and loses his own soul? Or what will a
man give in exchange for his soul? For the Son of Man
will come in the glory of His Father with His angels,
and then He will reward each according to his works.
"Assuredly, I say to you, there are some standing here
who shall not taste death till they see the Son of Man
coming in His kingdom." (Matthew 16:18-29)*

You see, we can have a spiritual awakening.

" Never forget that it's only the dead fish who swim with the stream."
— *Malcolm Muggeridge*

" I pray, then I obey."
— *David Yonggi Cho*

CHAPTER 37

Can a Christian
be Possessed?

For years, I taught a class on spiritual warfare in our Bible Training Center. As my tradition was, I would give the last ten to fifteen minutes of the class for Q&A. It never failed that this subject would come up. "Pastor Dick, can a believer be possessed?"

I would always answer this question with a question. "What kind of christian? A true, devout believer, like, say, Paul? Or, a casual, distant one who might show up at church on Christmas and Easter?" Both claim to be christian believers.

Most of my students would answer, "Well, someone who is serious about Christ, like those here in our class."

My answer to them was, "No, a true believer can never be totally controlled or owned by Satan or one of his soldiers, but they can be, as Dr. Ed Murphy says, 'demonized'".

Demon harassment is far different from possession. Okay, let's unwrap this. Let's first consider some scriptures:

Now whom you forgive anything, I also forgive. For if indeed I have forgiven anything, I have forgiven that one for your sakes in the presence of Christ, lest Satan should take advantage of us; for we are not ignorant of his devices. (2 Corinthians 2:10-11)

But refuse the younger widows; for when they have begun to grow wanton against Christ, they desire to marry, having condemnation because they have cast off their first faith. And besides they learn to be idle, wandering about from house to house, and not only idle but also gossips and busybodies, saying things which they ought not. Therefore I desire that the younger widows marry, bear children, manage the house, give no opportunity to the adversary to speak reproachfully. For some have already turned aside after Satan. (1 Timothy 5:11-15)

Paul talked about a spirit sent from Satan to afflict him. He called it a thorn in his flesh.

Jesus allowed Satan to sift Peter because of the fisherman's pride and self-indulgence. No wonder Peter later wrote:

Therefore humble yourselves under the mighty hand of God, that He may exalt you in due time, casting all your care upon Him, for He cares for you. Be sober, be vigilant; because your adversary the devil walks about like a roaring lion, seeking whom he may devour. Resist him, steadfast in the faith, knowing that the same suferings are experienced by your brotherhood in the world. But may the God of all grace, who called us to His eternal glory by Christ Jesus, after you have suffered a while, perfect, establish, strengthen, and settle you. (1 Peter 5:6-10)

As true believers, a demon is never allowed in our personal 'Holy of Holies." However, our spirit, our mind, our will, and our emotions can be infiltrated if we are not vigilant. Even our physical bodies can come under demonic attack at times.

Over the years I have cast out many an unclean spirit from pagans in India. I even cast a demon out of a cat in Oregon owned by a doctor. Yes, a cat! I thought he and his wife were joking until I went home with them and there it was – a huge demon possessed tabby cat. When it saw me it growled and lunged at me. I didn't think it was a joke for long. While the good doctor and his wife held it down, I performed deliverance on it and it worked. The cat calmed down and for the rest of its life was a fat, happy, mild, friendly, tabby cat. (Well, if pigs can be possessed, why not other animals?)

Once, I was preaching at a conference in Vancouver, Canada for some friends. As I walked around the front row and up one aisle, I said, "I have come tonight to challenge the powers of darkness."

A lady — middle-aged, matronly looking sister — stood up and screamed, then fainted. It was on that night I didn't get to preach or teach my message. It became a night of deliverance for several people. That church had never seen anything like it, nor had I, except on the mission field overseas.

Demons don't need passports to enter America or Canada. They may be harder to spot in western civilization. But believe me, they're here!

With the recent deluge of unspeakable crimes against family, children, and the innocent here in America, and the way our culture is swiftly shifting to an anti-biblical, anti-moral, anti-church, anti-Christ national view, it seems the demon kingdom is getting bolder and coming out of the shadows.

I had a member threaten to leave our church because his wife got upset over my six-week series on demonology and spiritual warfare. Being a big giver, he thought I would change course and get back to love, hope, and grace, which I had done many, many Sundays and still do. But those six weeks were too much for his wife.

I wonder what ever happened to that couple? I'm sure if they're still around they won't buy this book, but I still love them, and I'm still grateful for the support they showed while I preached what they wanted.

The truth is, our church grew while I ministered on warfare and demonstrated what I taught.

Don't ever think demons won't attend church. If demons are fallen angels (and there is no small debate over this), for the sake of argument, let's say they sometimes attend church. However, if they're attending church, they must miss the worship.

There are also religious spirits that believe they can dictate doctrine, or quench the Holy Spirit, and throw ice water on a service. Religious spirits love to criticize, condemn, get preachers to preach mad, and judge everyone about everything.

Religious spirits will help create false belief systems, cults, paganism, animism, and the like. I've had more than one visit from people with a religious spirit. They don't last long around Jubilee. I make sure of that.

I was holding a three-night meeting in the Chicago area. The Pastor was in need of an awakening. He was a good brother who had built a nice church. They had moved into a new facility after years of having a storefront church. The problem was the church had gotten tired, or "sleepy" as he put it.

"Dick, something has put a spirit of slumber over my congregation, and no matter what we do, it's not working. We've turned up the band; I tried preaching louder; all to no avail."

The first night I saw what he meant. The sanctuary was beautiful and had that "new look" to it, but he was right, the church looked dead! One elderly fellow was sound asleep at the end of the front row. I think I even heard him snoring.

Under my breath, I asked the Lord, "What's the problem here?"

He clearly said, "Look up at the ceiling."

Slowly, I lifted my eyes, and saw what looked like a big monkey sitting up there, staring at me. There it was! A spirit of slumber was dictating the flow of ministry and grinding it to a halt.

I yelled, "Come down from there now, in Jesus name." It instantly hopped down, slowly walked towards the back door leading out to the parking lot. Before it vanished, it turned and looked at me with a pitiful expression. Then slowly, shoulders slumped, and head down, it left.

That got folks attention. I shared what I saw, and the Pastor jumped up and shouted "Hallelujah!"

The old-timer who was asleep jumped up, lifted his hands, and began speaking in tongues.

Excitement swept through the crowd and revival broke out. What a meeting we had for three glorious nights.

The Pastor later told me the old fellow was a long-time member and elder in the church who was baptized in the spirit back in the 50s but had not spoken in tongues since that night.

What allowed that spirit entrance and to have a stronghold was not clear to the pastor, but he now knew how to watch and pray for any future gates to be opened, ignorantly or innocently.

CHAPTER 38

Be Careful Shopping

Lester Sumrall became famous for casting out two demons from a seventeen-year-old girl in the Philippines that bit her and left bloody teeth marks on her body. She would scream and say, "One is tall, the other is short and hairy, and they are hurting me!"

The local Catholic priest couldn't help her, so Dr. Sumrall got the call. After fasting and praying all night, he was ready. As soon as he entered the prison room one of the devils shouted, "We know who you are you, @$% bastard."

Ignoring their foul language, Doctor Sumrall went to work and set her free. She was wonderfully delivered and became a strong believer. This instantly became big news in Manila and spread, virtually around the world.

I traveled with Dr. Sumrall for years. He taught me much about demonology and how demons traffic. He shared a story about a teacher from England who had visited India and bought a vase with a snake on it. He thought it was unique and brought it to his classroom. He showed it to the students as he shared his trip. He later put it on the windowsill of the classroom. He didn't know that this brass vase that was shaped in the form of a coiled serpent had strange powers. Not knowing that demons can attach themselves to objects that are worshiped, he ignorantly thought it was just an interesting piece of art.

Not long after he displayed the vase, kids, started dozing off during class. He, himself, would get sleepy no matter what he did to stay alert. The demon-infested artifact was casting a spirit of slumber over the class.

I'm not sure if it was Dr. Sumrall or a colleague who warned the teacher — who was a believer, by the way — about the danger of displaying an object that could have been used in pagan worship.

The teacher took the vase down and tossed it in the garbage. And the classroom came alive again.

I have traveled the world since 1982, and one thing I've learned is to not bring home objects that could be a hiding place for demons.

Carla and I have dined with and ministered to many of our neighbors. One couple that was around our age adopted a teenage girl from Europe, who was raised in an orphanage. The adopted girl was attracted to my friend and began flirting with him, which freaked him out.

His wife thought it was normal for a blossoming teenager to have a crush on her handsome husband. But it made the man nervous, so he came to see me.

He was much more open to the Gospel than his wife. He wanted them all, the newly adopted daughter included, to attend Jubilee. They invited us over to dinner one night, and as we were sitting in their backyard, I noticed a big statue of Buddha in the garden. Of course, I commented on it asking where it came from.

My friend said, "Oh my wife found that and fell in love with it."

"Is she Buddhist?" I asked.

"Not a practicing one," he laughed out loud. "But she admires the philosophy of seeking inner peace."

Carla and I glanced at each other knowing here was a big part of the challenge.

Let me qualify something here, so we don't look for demons under every rock or live paranoid. I loved Dr. Cho's mother-in-law, whom we lovingly called, "Hallelujah Mama." She became a friend back in 1985 and introduced me to Dr. Cho. She taught prayer and fasting in our church many times and called me her American son. The last time I saw her was at our church in 1991. She ministered at our church and then passed away a few days later.

I loved her very much. However, her thoughts on demonology were extreme. She thought any object, doll, animal, teddy bear, and the like, were objects that attracted demons.

This caused Dr. Cho much grief. Once, she talked a member of Dr. Cho's church into destroying all her husband's expensive, jade, animal collection. The husband, not a believer, went into a rage and threatened to sue the church and to go public with its false teachings. What a mess!

She meant well, and to this day I love her, respect her, and honor her. She even had my picture glued inside her Bible next to her son-in-law, Dr. Cho. She was off target with her zeal to cleanse a house of everything she thought might attract demons.

No, we don't need to go on witch-hunts, but we do need to be watchful and discerning. Some things don't belong in our houses.

" You don't realize Jesus is all you need until Jesus is all you have."
— *Tim Keller*

CHAPTER 39

Serpents, Flies and Locusts

SERPENTS

Here, in the last book of the bible, we see our adversary called "...the dragon, that serpent of old who is the devil, Satan."

The first book of the bible, Genesis, gives us our first look at spiritual conflict — a conflict that took place in a perfect setting, in the Garden:

> *Now the serpent was more cunning than any beast of the field which the Lord God had made. And he said to the woman, "Has God indeed said, 'You shall not eat of every tree of the garden'?" And the woman said to the serpent, "We may eat the fruit of the trees of the garden; but of the fruit of the tree which is in the midst of the garden, God has said, 'You shall not eat it, nor shall you touch it, lest you die.'" Then the serpent said to the woman, "You will not surely die. (Genesis 3:1-4)*

Satan, an invisible creature, needed to possess a body to begin his dialogue with Eve. The serpent, a naturally cunning and skilled creature, even to this very day, was obviously no threat to Eve for she willingly engaged in conversation.

So the Lord God said to the serpent: "Because you have done this, You are cursed more than all cattle, and more than every beast of the field; On your belly you shall go, And you shall eat dust All the days of your life. And I will put enmity between you and the woman, and between your seed and her Seed; He shall bruise your head, and you shall bruise His heel." (Genesis 3:14-15)

As we touched on earlier, how Satan was able to enter the serpent is not clear. If demons could inhabit any animal at anytime it would be chaos. Why he picked this creature is a little more obvious.

Finding Eve somewhat isolated, he smoothly moves in with cunning and deceit. Snakes today are some of the most patient, stealthy hunters. They are colored to blend in with their environment. More than once out in the field, hiking, hunting, or fishing I've nearly stepped on a snake, even dangerous rattlers.

Bill Johnson, of Bethel Church in Redding, California, is an avid outdoorsman. He shared how up in Northern California there are old rock boundary fences created in the Nineteenth Century by Chinese laborers. If needing to climb over on of these three to four-foot high rock fences, you should first make a noise to alert any rattlers hiding in the cracks.

Snakes know how to hide and hunt. Paul found this out the hard way while picking up sticks to warm himself by a fire after a shipwreck.

FLIES

Then the multitude came together again, so that they could not so much as eat bread. But when His own people heard about this, they went out to lay hold of Him, for they said, "He is out of His mind." And the scribes who came down from Jerusalem said, "He has Beelzebub," and, "By the ruler of the demons He casts out demons." So He called them to Himself and said to them in parables: "How can Satan cast out Satan? If a kingdom is divided against itself, that kingdom cannot stand. And if a house is divided against itself, that house cannot stand. And if Satan has risen up against himself, and is divided, he cannot stand, but has an end. No one can enter a strong man's house and plunder his goods, unless he first binds the strong man. And then he will plunder his house. (Mark 3:20-27)

Jesus is accused of driving out demons by the power of Beelzebub, a powerful prince of demons. This account is also recorded in Matthew and Luke. Beelzebub is also called "The Lord of the Flies" or "Lord of the dung heap." This title came from one of the ancient books of the Old Testament:

But the angel of the Lord said to Elijah the Tishbite, "Arise, go up to meet the messengers of the king of Samaria, and say to them, 'Is it because there is no God in Israel that you are going to inquire of Baal-Zebub, the god of Ekron?'" (2 Kings 1:3)

Baal (Beel) means *Lord*. The god of Ekron was derogatorily called *the lord of dung that attracts flies*.

285

Beelzebub is thought by many to be a high-ranking prince in Satan's army. John Milton, in his book, *Paradise Lost*, had Beelzebub ranked as the second most powerful demon. John Bunyan also mentioned this demon in his book, *The Pilgrim's Progress*.

Once, when I was teaching a class on demonology, I told the students, "If you want to get insight into the trafficking of demons, study flies!"

A fly's scientific name is *Diptera*, which is a Greek word meaning *two wings*. Demons swarm like flies. The atmosphere is their realm, and they are attracted to garbage, dumpsters, and dead things.

Some flies bite. I know about that first-hand because I've been bitten by horse flies several times.

Not only are flies attracted to dead things, but that's also where they lay their eggs and produce maggots. To see a dead animal full of maggots is a hellish sight and the smell is hard to forget.

As flies are attracted to wounds and open sores, demons likewise are drawn to inner turmoil, unforgiveness, bitterness, racism, and every shade of hatred.

LOCUSTS

The eighth plague in Egypt was the plague of locusts:

So Moses stretched out his rod over the land of Egypt, and the Lord brought an east wind on the land all that day and all that night. When it was morning, the east wind brought the locusts. And the locusts went up over all the land of Egypt and rested on all the territory of Egypt. They were very severe; previously there had been no such locusts as they, nor shall there be such after them. For they covered the face of the whole earth, so that the land was darkened; and they ate every herb of the land and all the fruit of the trees which the hail had left. So there remained nothing green on the trees or on the plants of the field throughout all the land of Egypt. (Exodus 10:13-15)

In the book of Revelation we read:

Then out of the smoke locusts came upon the earth. And to them was given power, as the scorpions of the earth have power. They were commanded not to harm the grass of the earth, or any green thing, or any tree, but only those men who do not have the seal of God on their foreheads. And they were not given authority to kill them, but to torment them for five months. Their torment was like the torment of a scorpion when it strikes a man. In those days men will seek death and will not find it; they will desire to die, and death will flee from them. The shape of the locusts was like horses prepared for battle. On their heads were crowns of something like gold, and their faces were like the faces of men. They had hair like women's hair, and their teeth were like lions' teeth. And they had breastplates like breastplates of iron, and the sound of their wings was like the sound of chariots with many horses running into battle. They had tails like scorpions, and there were stings in their tails. Their power was to hurt men five months. (Revelation 9:3-10)

The bible has many stories of the destruction created by swarms of locusts. In the book of Joel, swarms of locust devastate the crops and economy of Israel. Demons, like hordes of swarming grasshoppers on steroids, would love to devastate our families, cities, and our nation:

What the chewing locust left, the swarming locust has eaten; What the swarming locust left, the crawling locust has eaten; And what the crawling locust left, the consuming locust has eaten. (Joel 1:4)

The locusts, like demons, have various skills. Joel mentions the chewing ones, the swarming ones, the crawling ones, and the consuming horde. In chapters one and two of the book of Joel, he talks about a horrible day of judgment, but with hope:

"Now, therefore," says the Lord, "Turn to Me with all your heart, With fasting, with weeping, and with mourning." So rend your heart, and not your garments; Return to the Lord your God, For He is gracious and merciful, Slow to anger, and of great kindness; And He relents from doing harm. Who knows if He will turn and relent, And leave a blessing behind Him — A grain offering and a drink offering For the Lord your God? Blow the trumpet in Zion, Consecrate a fast, Call a sacred assembly; Gather the people, Sanctify the congregation, Assemble the

elders, Gather the children and nursing babes; Let the bridegroom go out from his chamber, And the bride from her dressing room. Let the priests, who minister to the Lord, Weep between the porch and the altar; Let them say, "Spare Your people, O Lord, And do not give Your heritage to reproach, That the nations should rule over them. Why should they say among the peoples, 'Where is their God?'" (Joel 2:12-17)

On the day of Pentecost, the Holy Spirit used a passage from Joel 2:28-32, to launch God's new, Spirit-filled ecclesia — the church of Jesus Christ.

Just like pests, insects, or serpents, satan and his evil cadre have predictable patterns. Let's not over-estimate Satan. He's limited, even though Hollywood and superstition would paint him as all-powerful. On the other hand, let's not underestimate satan. He's an evil genius. He is the father of lies and deception. He has perfected his strategies and wiles, as Paul called it. With Eve he brings Gods word into question.

He doesn't deny there is a God. He subtly inserts doubt as to God's integrity. He used this old tactic with David:

Now Satan stood up against Israel, and moved David to number Israel. And God was displeased with this thing; therefore He struck Israel. So David said to God, "I have sinned greatly, because I have done this thing; but now, I pray, take away the iniquity of Your servant, for I have done very foolishly." (1 Chronicles 21:7-8)

Later, Satan challenged the Sonship of Jesus, His calling, and His resolve to go the distance on the hard road that God had chosen for Him to walk by suggesting an easy solution, "Just bow to me once, and all this world is yours".

In similar fashion, He sent a thorn to the flesh of Paul and sifted Peter *like wheat.*

Satan targets leaders: Parents, Kings, Prophets, Apostles, Pastors and church leaders. Don't get me wrong, he hates all humanity, but he focuses on leadership.

He will sow tares amongst the healthy wheat of our churches and cause church splits, jealousy, immorality, and bad or false doctrine. We need to be vigilant, watch and pray, and keep an eye out for our relentless enemy who walks around like a roaring lion.

While I was in Africa on one of my mission trips, Carla and I took a few days off to go on a safari in Kruger National Park in South Africa. At dinner one night, which was in a fenced in outdoor area, we heard a roar in the darkness. It had a pitiful sound to it.

I asked our guide, Steve, "What was that?"

"Oh, that's an old lion who has been cast out of his pride and is losing his strength and most of his teeth. His only way to hunt is to roar and hopefully scare game his way as he hides in the tall grass."

I instantly thought of Satan. He was kicked out of heaven, and he lost his pride.

CHAPTER 40

Paul and the Gentile World

Then Saul, still breathing threats and murder against the disciples of the Lord, went to the high priest and asked letters from him to the synagogues of Damascus, so that if he found any who were of the Way, whether men or women, he might bring them bound to Jerusalem. As he journeyed he came near Damascus, and suddenly a light shone around him from heaven. Then he fell to the ground, and heard a voice saying to him, "Saul, Saul, why are you persecuting Me?" And he said, "Who are You, Lord?" Then the Lord said, "I am Jesus, whom you are persecuting. It is hard for you to kick against the goads." So he, trembling and astonished, said, "Lord, what do You want me to do?" Then the Lord said to him, "Arise and go into the city, and you will be told what you must do." (Acts 9:1-6)

But the Lord said to him, "Go, for he is a chosen vessel of Mine to bear My name before Gentiles, kings, and the children of Israel. (Acts 9:15)

Paul, who, when he was Saul, was a Jewish, religious intellectual with unbridled zeal for the Law of Moses. He was God's main man to bring the story, the name and the power of Jesus to a world steeped in Greco-Roman culture, religious beliefs and lifestyle.

Traveling the world as I have for well over thirty-six years, I've seen people's vain attempts to appease or ward off evil spirits with masks of grotesque figures, carvings, and statues lining rooftops, amulets, fetishes, and other practices of magic. I've witnessed voodoo workers, Hindu temples, Buddhist temples, Sooth Sayers, and palm readers, peeps, wizards, and the list goes on. All of these people believe in the supernatural and in the invisible realm of spirits, good and bad, and they are trying to make peace with evil.

Paul would bring his message to such a world. The book of Acts records much of it, which is a great help to us, now, on how to deal with the powers of darkness. Satan, of course, recognized Paul's anointing and mission. He would try his best to derail the great apostle, if not kill him, or at least stop him, and maybe discourage him.

Paul's adventure begins:

> *Now in the church that was at Antioch there were certain prophets and teachers: Barnabas, Simeon who was called Niger, Lucius of Cyrene, Manaen who had been brought up with Herod the tetrarch, and Saul. As they ministered to the Lord and fasted, the Holy Spirit said, "Now separate to Me Barnabas and Saul for the*

work to which I have called them." Then, having fasted and prayed, and laid hands on them, they sent them away. So, being sent out by the Holy Spirit, they went down to Seleucia, and from there they sailed to Cyprus. And when they arrived in Salamis, they preached the word of God in the synagogues of the Jews. They also had John as their assistant. Now when they had gone through the island to Paphos, they found a certain sorcerer, a false prophet, a Jew whose name was Bar-Jesus. (Acts 13:1-6)

It would not take long for Paul to engage in spiritual warfare. Let's keep reading:

Who was with the proconsul, Sergius Paulus, an intelligent man. This man called for Barnabas and Saul and sought to hear the word of God. But Elymas the sorcerer (for so his name is translated) withstood them, seeking to turn the proconsul away from the faith. Then Saul, who also is called Paul, filled with the Holy Spirit, looked intently at him and said, "O full of all deceit and all fraud, you son of the devil, you enemy of all righteousness, will you not cease perverting the straight ways of the Lord? And now, indeed, the hand of the Lord is upon you, and you shall be blind, not seeing the sun for a time." And immediately a dark mist fell on him, and he went around seeking someone to lead him by the hand. Then the proconsul believed, when he saw what had been done, being astonished at the teaching of the Lord. (Acts 7-12)

Being somewhat of an old fashioned Full Gospel preacher-teacher, planted in the heart of Silicon Valley, surrounded by left-leaning, humanistic, socialist influences, I'm more than ever convinced it's going to take more than a "cool church" with snappy programs and good sermons to win my region to Christ.

Paul didn't win this battle by out arguing or debating. He released God's power and shut satan up! When the proconsul saw what had been done, he became a believer.

This must have freaked satan out! Rattled or not, he would not quit because the devil doesn't know what else to do because he is out of his mind with hatred towards God and God's people:

> *So when the Jews went out of the synagogue, the Gentiles begged that these words might be preached to them the next Sabbath. Now when the congregation had broken up, many of the Jews and devout proselytes followed Paul and Barnabas, who, speaking to them, persuaded them to continue in the grace of God. On the next Sabbath almost the whole city came together to hear the word of God. But when the Jews saw the multitudes, they were filled with envy; and contradicting and blaspheming, they opposed the things spoken by Paul. Then Paul and Barnabas grew bold and said, "It was necessary that the word of God should be spoken to you first; but since you reject it, and judge yourselves unworthy of everlasting life, behold, we turn to the Gentiles. For so the Lord has commanded us: 'I have set you as a*

light to the Gentiles, That you should be for salvation to the ends of the earth."' Now when the Gentiles heard this, they were glad and glorified the word of the Lord. And as many as had been appointed to eternal life believed. And the word of the Lord was being spread throughout all the region. But the Jews stirred up the devout and prominent women and the chief men of the city, raised up persecution against Paul and Barnabas, and expelled them from their region. But they shook off the dust from their feet against them, and came to Iconium. And the disciples were filled with joy and with the Holy Spirit. (Acts 13:42-52)

In Antioch, Paul learned that we win some and we lose some. However, we must keep preaching the truth even if Satan is stirring up closed-minded people.

Next stop, Iconium:

Now it happened in Iconium that they went together to the synagogue of the Jews, and so spoke that a great multitude both of the Jews and of the Greeks believed. But the unbelieving Jews stirred up the Gentiles and poisoned their minds against the brethren. Therefore they stayed there a long time, speaking boldly in the Lord, who was bearing witness to the word of His grace, granting signs and wonders to be done by their hands. But the multitude of the city was divided: part sided with the Jews, and part with the apostles. And when a violent attempt was made by both the Gentiles and Jews, with their rulers, to abuse and stone them, they became aware of it and fled to Lystra and Derbe, cities of Lycaonia, and to the surrounding region. And they were preaching the gospel there. (Acts 14:1-7)

It gets worse!

Then Jews from Antioch and Iconium came there; and having persuaded the multitudes, they stoned Paul and dragged him out of the city, supposing him to be dead. However, when the disciples gathered around him, he rose up and went into the city. And the next day he departed with Barnabas to Derbe. (Acts 14:19-20)

I love the next two verses:

And when they had preached the gospel to that city and made many disciples, they returned to Lystra, Iconium, and Antioch, strengthening the souls of the disciples, exhorting them to continue in the faith, and saying, "We must through many tribulations enter the kingdom of God." (Acts 14:21-22)

There is no fear in our hero's of the faith! One account that needs our scrutiny is found in the sixteenth chapter of Acts:

Now it happened, as we went to prayer, that a certain slave girl possessed with a spirit of divination met us, who brought her masters much profit by fortune-telling. This girl followed Paul and us, and cried out, saying, "These men are the servants of the Most High God, who proclaim to us the way of salvation." And this she did for many days. But Paul, greatly annoyed, turned and said to the spirit, "I command you in the name of Jesus Christ to come out of her." And he came out that very hour. But when her masters saw that their hope of profit was gone, they seized Paul and Silas and dragged them into the marketplace to the authorities. And they brought them to the magistrates, and said, "These men, being Jews, exceedingly trouble our city; and they teach customs which are not lawful for us, being Romans, to receive or observe." Then the multitude rose up together against them; and the magistrates tore off their clothes and commanded them to be beaten with rods. And when they had laid many stripes on them, they threw them into prison, commanding the jailer to keep them securely. Having received such a charge, he put them into the inner prison and fastened their feet in the stocks. (Acts 16:16-24)

Here, among the Philippians, Paul is confronted by the spirit of *Phythos* (python), which had control over this poor slave girl who had brought much financial gain to her owners by portraying herself as an oracle of God.

The word divination, in our text, is *pythos* — a huge constrictor snake. That's why she was referred to as a priestess or pythoness. According to their superstitions, she was a prophetess of the Greek god Apollo, who was worshiped at the shrine of Delphi in Greece.

The python kills its prey by squeezing out breath and life with its strength. The *spirit of python* is still around today. It tries to squeeze the life out of the local church and ministries. It works hand in hand with the spirit of Jezebel, using flattery, deception, partial truth. That's what this girl was doing when she advertised Paul and his team as "Servants of the most high God."

The spirit of divination promised selfish gain, which was common for mediums back in Paul's day. It's the same today with fortunetellers and psychics:

> *And this she did for many days. But Paul, greatly annoyed, turned and said to the spirit, "I command you in the name of Jesus Christ to come out of her." And he came out that very hour. But when her masters saw that their hope of profit was gone, they seized Paul and Silas and dragged them into the marketplace to the authorities. (Acts 14:18-19)*

It took Paul a while to discern her tactics, but once the lights came on our hero went to work. Religious spirits are the most difficult to detect because they will come across as very humble and spiritual until their opportunity to gain a foothold unfolds. Then the mask comes off!

A Pastor friend of mine in Australia had a very gifted worship leader whom I enjoyed tremendously when I visited and spoke at his amazing church. My last time there, I said, "Hey, where is brother so and so?"

My friend dropped his head in silence and looked up with a pained expression. "The mask came off." He went on to share how this very gifted man had a spirit of Jezebel and ran off any and all competition.

My friend began noticing members leaving the music department and going to another church. When he confronted his worship leader, he would simply say, "Oh, they were impossible to work with and weren't anointed enough to play or sing."

The Pastor started looking into the matter and he discovered the problem was his music guy had a controlling, python spirit that ran off good people because he was afraid he might lose control of the music department.

As much as the Pastor liked his worship leader, he had to confront him. That's when the mask came off. It was like another personality took over, and it was ugly. I felt bad for my friend because he truly loved the guy.

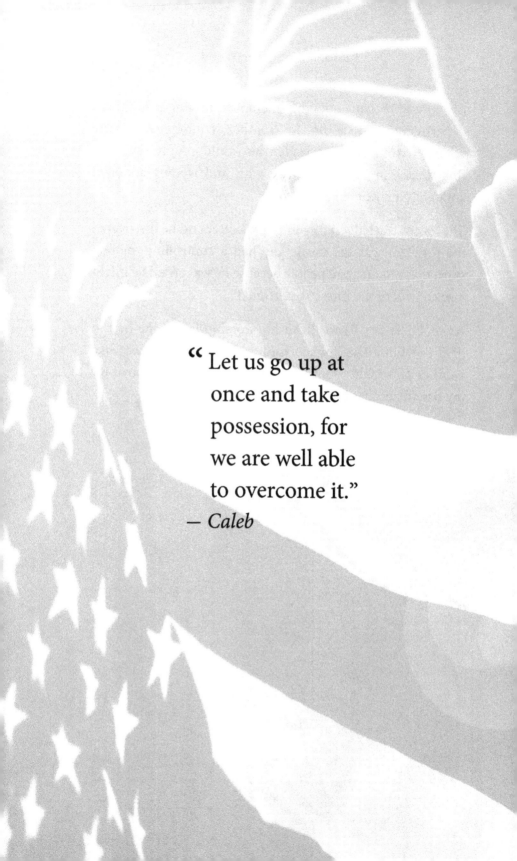

" Let us go up at once and take possession, for we are well able to overcome it."
— *Caleb*

CHAPTER 41

Cities Can Be Won

My favorite book in the Pauline Epistles is his letter to the Ephesians. These are rich in content: Chapter 1, *Who we are in Christ;* Chapter 2, *Where we are in Christ;* Chapter 3, *Why we are in Christ.*

These are the *In Him* realities that Paul's letters speak of: Chapter 4, *Walk in Unity;* Chapter 5, *Walk in love;* Chapter 6, *Honor, obedience, and warfare.*

Paul's missionary trip to the hip, modern, active city of Ephesus is found here:

> *And it happened, while Apollos was at Corinth, that Paul, having passed through the upper regions, came to Ephesus. And finding some disciples, he said to them, "Did you receive the Holy Spirit when you believed?" So they said to him, "We have not so much as heard whether there is a Holy Spirit." And he said to them, "Into what then were you baptized?" So they said, "Into John's baptism." Then Paul said, "John indeed baptized with a baptism of repentance, saying to the people that*

they should believe on Him who would come after him, that is, on Christ Jesus." When they heard this, they were baptized in the name of the Lord Jesus. And when Paul had laid hands on them, the Holy Spirit came upon them, and they spoke with tongues and prophesied. Now the men were about twelve in all. (Acts 19:1-7)

Ephesus was a very important port city and a major trade center of the ancient world. It was located on Turkey's western coast. Nearly 300,000 people lived there at its height and glory. The city's claim to fame was its temple to the goddess Artemis (Diana), one of the seven wonders of the ancient world. The religious zeal and money made from it would be a challenge for Paul and his newly acquired, twelve, freshly-baptized-with-the-spirit followers.

Paul clearly understood this stronghold city would need a power encounter with Spirit-filled followers:

Now God worked unusual miracles by the hands of Paul so that even handkerchiefs or aprons were brought from his body to the sick, and the diseases left them and the evil spirits went out of them. Then some of the itinerant Jewish exorcists took it upon themselves to call the name of the Lord Jesus over those who had evil spirits, saying, "We exorcise you by the Jesus whom Paul preaches." Also there were seven sons of Sceva, a Jewish chief priest, who did so. And the evil spirit answered and said, "Jesus I know, and Paul I know; but who are you?" Then the man in whom the evil spirit was leaped on them, overpowered them, and prevailed against them, so that they fled out of that house naked and wounded. This became known both to all Jews and Greeks dwelling in Ephesus; and fear fell on them all, and the name of the Lord Jesus was magnified. 18 And many who had believed came confessing and telling their deeds. Also, many of those who had practiced magic brought their books together and burned them in the sight of all. And they counted up the value of them, and it totaled fifty thousand pieces of silver. So the word of the Lord grew mightily and prevailed. (Acts 19:11-20)

A city like Ephesus would not be impacted with clever, thirty-minute sermons. When I visit San Francisco, forty-five minutes north of San Jose, I think of Ephesus. These two cities are, in many ways, much alike. Both Ancient Ephesus and modern San Francisco are major port cities, which have a mixture of race, culture, and languages that vary from block-to-block.

The story of the itinerant, Jewish exorcists is worth studying. These Jews, the sons of a religious figure named Sceva. These vagabond exorcists made a living doing this. In those days, most illnesses and sickness were attributed to evil spirits, so they had plenty of work. How successful they were is unknown.

With Paul's newfound fame spreading throughout the city, these boys were impressed with his results, and they thought they had found a new method. Using our Lord's name, and even Paul's name, as if there was some kind of magical power attached, proved near fatal. In this Hellenistic world, magic held a place of esteem in the eyes of the citizens. The mixing of spiritualism and magic was in vogue.

When the seven exorcists saw what a handkerchief and even common aprons could do by being exposed to Paul's body, they must have thought, "Now this is magic!" Obviously, hearing about Jesus from Paul's messages, they figured maybe a little of the magic dust would fall on them.

How these Jewish men, with Dad's permission, mixed magic with traditional beliefs is uncertain.

Today, we see Catholicism as a mixture of biblical accuracy and old pagan beliefs.

It also amazes me how contemporary christian leaders want to wear Jewish prayer shawls, hold Saturday services, and take us back to the Old Testament. It's easy to see how people can mix sound doctrine with superstition, especially if it sells.

Jewish exorcists were not unique to these seven:

> *Then one was brought to Him who was demon-possessed, blind and mute; and He healed him, so that the blind and mute man both spoke and saw. And all the multitudes were amazed and said, "Could this be the Son of David?" Now when the Pharisees heard it they said, "This fellow does not cast out demons except by Beelzebub, the ruler of the demons." But Jesus knew their thoughts, and said to them: "Every kingdom divided against itself is brought to desolation, and every city or house divided against itself will not stand.*

If Satan casts out Satan, he is divided against himself. How then will his kingdom stand? And if I cast out demons by Beelzebub, by whom do your sons cast them out? Therefore they shall be your judges. But if I cast out demons by the Spirit of God, surely the kingdom of God has come upon you. (Matthew 12:22-28)

What stands out in this story is that satan and his demons know who is real and who isn't. Jesus, no doubt, is real. They knew who the Lord was. Oh, they knew who Paul was, too. But the devils showed no respect for the seven wannabees. I wonder if the Sons of Sceva learned anything from this?

Then the man in whom the evil spirit was leaped on them, overpowered them, and prevailed against them, so that they fled out of that house naked and wounded. (Acts 19:16)

You might practice magic, play around and experiment with occult-like things without ever using the Lord's name. However, you'll loose the battle if you're not truly His and if you're not genuinely prepared.

Throughout the remainder of the Book of Acts, Paul typically had either a revival or a riot. Power ministries stir things up, both good and bad.

It was one thing to mess with their religion, but to mess with their money? That went too far.

Diana, or Artemis was the goddess of fertility and the hunt, like Minerva, and the goddess of the Cosmos. She was also called the goddess of the moon. The demon principality that was receiving worship behind the image of Diana had to be extremely upset over Paul's intrusion into its domain. This whole region was demonized, and many people were demon possessed.

We see, again, under Paul's influence and ministry, demon spirits went out of many. It was power warfare that opened Ephesus to the Gospel of Christ.

I'm not against an entertaining church with slick marketing and cool, attractive programs, but not at the expense of power-church!

Why compromise? We can have it all!

" The Church is the gate of heaven."
— *Bill Johnson*

CHAPTER 42

What's In a Name?

A few years back, I was with my grandson Nicholas who was around five years old at the time. I asked, "Nick, what's Grandpa's name?"

He answered without hesitation, "Pastor."

I laughed so loud it startled him. "No, Nick it's Richard William Bernal or Dick Bernal."

He frowned a bit, and said, "No, it's Pastor! Everyone calls you Pastor."

"Well, yes, that's true Nick. But that's my title, not my name."

He looked puzzled, so I began sharing how I became Pastor Dick and where I got my name, Richard William Bernal. I was named after Richard Phelps, my Uncle Dick from my Mother's side of the family, and William, after my Dad and Grandpa, both of whom were known as Bill.

In studying the Bible, we see the importance of names, in particular, the names of God.

Name: *A word or phrase by which a person or thing is designated; That which identifies a person, place, or thing.*

In Ana Spangler's book, *Praying the Names of God*, she lists
the following names:

- **Ab, Abba** – *Father*
- **Adonay** – *Lord*
- **Ebed Yahweh** – *Servant of the Lord*
- **Ehyeh** – *I am*
- **El, Elohim, Eloah** – *God*
- **El Chay** – *Living God*
- **El Elyon** – *God Most High*
- **El Kanna** – *Jealous god*
- **El Olam** – *Everlasting God, Eternal God*
- **El Roi** – *the God Who Watches Over Me*
- **El Shaddai** – *God Almighty*
- **Esh Oklah** – *Consuming Fire*
- **Go'el** – *Redeemer, Defender*
- **Hashem** – *the Name*
- **Immanuel** – *God with Us*
- **Ish** – *Husband*
- **Ish Makoboth** – *Man of Sorrows*
- **Machseh** – *Refuge*
- **Magen** – *Sheild*
- **Maon** – *Dwelling Place*
- **Mashiach** – *Christ, Messiah*
- **Melek** – *King*
- **Metsuda** – *Fortress*
- **Migdal-Oz** – *Strong Tower*
- **Miqweh Yisrael** – *Hope of Israel*
- **Qedosh Yisrael** – *Holy One of Israel*

- **Rabbi, Rabbouni** – *Teacher*
- **Ruach** – *Spirit*
- **Ruach El** – *God's Spirit*
- **Ruach Elohim** – *the Spirit of God*
- **Ruach Qodesh** – *Holy Spirit*
- **Ruach Yahweh** – *the Lord's Spirit*
- **Sar Shalom** – *Prince of Peace*
- **Shopet** – *Judge*
- **Tsemach** – *Branch*
- **Yah, Yahweh** – *Lord*
- **Yahweh Nissi** – *the Lord My Banner*
- **Yahweh Roi** – *the Lord is My Shepherd*
- **Yahweh Ropheka** – *the Lord Who Heals*
- **Yahweh Shalom** – *the Lord is Peace*
- **Yahweh Shammah** – *the Lord Is There*
- **Yahweh Tseboath** – *Lord Almighty, the Lord of Armies, The Lord of Hosts*
- **Yahweh Tsidqenu** – *the Lord Our Righteousness*
- **Yahweh Tsur** – *the Lord My Rock*
- **Yahweh Yireh** – *the Lord Will Provide*
- **Yeshua** – *Jesus*

The Bible is a book of progressive revelation. Every book expresses a clearer picture of God and the Lord Jesus as we go from Genesis to Revelation.

What's wonderful is all these names point to one...Jesus!

In spiritual warfare, it's imperative we know our enemy. His names and titles give us insight into his plans and schemes to destroy mankind.

My friend Bishop Tudor Bismark wrote this for his 2015 National Prayer Summit — *The Chain of Command in the Demonic Realm*:

Demons are very conscious of authority and adhere to the chain of command and the line of authority structure. There are Chief Kings and Chief Princes, and under them are Kings and Princes, and under them are Kings and Princes who rule various geographical and spiritual areas. There are kingdoms, principalities, dominions, and powers, which are administered by Kings and Princes. Each state in the United States is ruled over by a prince.

A General is in charge of a Legion (6,000), while a Prince will control a number of Legions.

A Ruler of Captains commands a Cohort (600), and there can be Chief Captains and Chief Rulers with still more authority.

A Centurion controls 100 demons. If he controls fewer than a hundred demons he is called a Strongman

Any demon in authority will direct how many, when, and where pain spirits are to attack, and how sustained the attack is to be. Those in charge call these pain spirits Imps. Because of the rigid authority structure, a wise move in dealing with spirits is to bind all spirits, especially ruling ones and ones of Violence, Fighting, and Murder.

The control of a geographical area seems to rest on the success of a prince in controlling the majority of the persons within that place. It also has to do with the ferocity and power of that prince.

I'm convinced that satan modeled his kingdom after God's. Demons are very aware of authority, and, I'm sure, obey out of fear of their evil master. Paul gives us some insight into this in his letter to the Ephesians:

> *Finally, my brethren, be strong in the Lord and in the power of His might. Put on the whole armor of God, that you may be able to stand against the wiles of the devil. For we do not wrestle against flesh and blood, but against principalities, against powers, against the rulers of the darkness of this age, against spiritual hosts of wickedness in the heavenly places. (Ephesians 6:10-12)*

Likewise, as regions and nations have angelic princes and rulers, consider this:

> *In those days I, Daniel, was mourning three full weeks. I ate no pleasant food, no meat or wine came into my mouth, nor did I anoint myself at all, till three whole weeks were fulfilled. Now on the twenty-fourth day of the first month, as I was by the side of the great river, that is, the Tigris, I lifted my eyes and looked, and behold, a certain man clothed in linen, whose waist was girded with gold of Uphaz! His body was like beryl, his face like the appearance of lightning, his eyes like torches of fire, his arms and feet like burnished bronze*

in color, and the sound of his words like the voice of a multitude. And I, Daniel, alone saw the vision, for the men who were with me did not see the vision; but a great terror fell upon them, so that they fled to hide themselves. Therefore I was left alone when I saw this great vision, and no strength remained in me; for my vigor was turned to frailty in me, and I retained no strength. Yet I heard the sound of his words; and while I heard the sound of his words I was in a deep sleep on my face, with my face to the ground. Suddenly, a hand touched me, which made me tremble on my knees and on the palms of my hands. And he said to me, "O Daniel, man greatly beloved, understand the words that I speak to you, and stand upright, for I have now been sent to you." While he was speaking this word to me, I stood trembling. Then he said to me, "Do not fear, Daniel, for from the first day that you set your heart to understand, and to humble yourself before your God, your words were heard; and I have come because of your words. But the prince of the kingdom of Persia withstood me twenty-one days; and behold, Michael, one of the chief princes, came to help me, for I had been left alone there with the kings of Persia. Now I have come to make you understand what will happen to your people in the latter days, for the vision refers to many days yet to come." When he had spoken such words to me, I turned my face toward the ground and became speechless. And suddenly, one having the likeness of the sons of men touched my lips; then I opened my mouth and spoke, saying to him who stood before me, "My lord, because of the vision my sorrows

*have overwhelmed me, and I have retained no strength.
For how can this servant of my lord talk with you, my
lord? As for me, no strength remains in me now, nor is
any breath left in me." Then again, the one having the
likeness of a man touched me and strengthened me. 19
And he said, "O man greatly beloved, fear not! Peace be
to you; be strong, yes, be strong!" So when he spoke to
me I was strengthened, and said, "Let my lord speak,
for you have strengthened me." Then he said, "Do you
know why I have come to you? And now I must return
to fight with the prince of Persia; and when I have gone
forth, indeed the prince of Greece will come. But I will
tell you what is noted in the Scripture of Truth. No one
upholds me against these, except Michael your prince.
(Daniel 10:2-21)*

Wow! Here's a rare glimpse of cosmic warfare. God's
messenger angel, probably Gabriel, was sent by God to
deliver a prophetic word to Daniel, who was fasting (which
is a vital weapon of warfare). But a demonic prince called the
Prince of Persia, a prince who yet controls a big part of the
Middle East today, held up the angel for twenty-one days.

Michael, the war-angel was dispatched by heaven to help
Gabriel break through and bring God's word to Daniel. I'm
convinced Gabriel would have turned around and gone back
home to heaven if Daniel had broken his fast.

We also see another demonic prince, the Prince of Greece,
rising up to take over for the defeated Prince of Persia, or, at
the very least, to lend a demonic hand.

Over the years, I've conducted countless seminars and sermons on territorial spirits, both angelic and demonic. I believe both the heavenly host and satan's cadre are given areas to rule, or to protect, or to set up evil strongholds — seats of authority and rule, if you will.

Look at this amazing passage from Revelation:

> "And to the angel of the church in Pergamos write, 'These things says He who has the sharp two-edged sword: "I know your works, and where you dwell, where Satan's throne is. And you hold fast to My name, and did not deny My faith even in the days in which Antipas was My faithful martyr, who was killed among you, where Satan dwells. (Revelation 2:12-13)

Where Satan's throne is? Some suggest Pergamos was a city built on the ruins of ancient Troy. Pergamos was a corrupt city, and corrupt men infiltrated this struggling church that John wrote about:

> But I have a few things against you, because you have there those who hold the doctrine of Balaam, who taught Balak to put a stumbling block before the children of Israel, to eat things sacrificed to idols, and to commit sexual immorality. Thus you also have those who hold the doctrine of the Nicolaitans, which thing I hate. Repent, or else I will come to you quickly and will fight against them with the sword of My mouth. "He who has an ear, let him hear what the Spirit says to the churches. To him who overcomes I will give some of the hidden manna to eat. And I will give him a white

stone, and on the stone a new name written which no one knows except him who receives it.'" (Revelations 2:14-17)

The good people of this church were struggling, but they were still holding fast to that which was true and good.

Here's the point to remember: Satan sets up seats of government where there is wickedness, cruelty, and error.

WATER SPIRITS

Several years ago a Pastor friend, Larry Huggins, who lived in San Francisco at the time, had a pastor from Nigeria, Africa, visiting and ministering at his church that we helped plant. Dr. Huggins decided to take his Nigerian friend to the city of Santa Cruz, a beautiful coastal resort town here in the Bay Area. It's a place I know well, as I spent much of my youth hanging out surfing, swimming, sunbathing, and having fun.

As Larry drove closer to the ocean, the Nigerian pastor yelled, "Stop, stop, stop! Please, Pastor, pullover. Let's go back!"

My friend, Larry, was perplexed. He asked, "Are you ok?"

The missionary said, "There are too many water spirits here, very strong, very wicked, please let's go back!"

When I heard the story, it got me thinking about what he saw, why, and why Santa Cruz?

Santa Cruz is known as the Lesbian capital of Northern California. Also, after the 1967-1969 Hippie movement died down in San Francisco, many hippies moved to Santa Cruz, forty miles down the coast.

In my research, I found something fascinating: local Indian tribes who caught women having sex with other women banished them to the Santa Cruz area. Their encampment was at the mouth of the San Lorenzo river which dumps into the Pacific at Santa Cruz. If you ever visit the Santa Cruz boardwalk, notice the river is at the south end of the walk. That's the San Lorenzo River where the ancient, Native American, lesbian encampment was located.

I'm not sure what the African minister saw but this I know, preachers in Africa are more discerning to the demonic world than most western preachers. They live among the ancient forms of occult and pagan worship, which still exists today in Africa. It makes them more alert and insightful.

We need to become more alert of the realm of the demonic if we want the kingdom of God to expand.

Another man I love talking with about this topic is Bishop Tudor Bismark of Zimbabwe, Africa. His knowledge of demonic activity is amazing.

In our opening narrative, we saw Jesus telling us what happens once a demon is evicted and found homeless:

> *When an unclean spirit goes out of a man, he goes through dry places, seeking rest, and finds none. (Matthew 12:43)*

Notice, the restless, irritated demon is in a dry place or waterless place. A dry place could mean a desert or a deserted place where very few people live and there is little opportunity to do mischief or find a new home. Demons are only satisfied if they can inhabit a body and harm it as much as they can.

The larger part of humanity lives near water. The biggest, most important, economic centers are cities situated along the coast of an ocean or a major, navigable river. Obviously, demons don't want to be exiled to a dry wilderness.

I'm not sure what kind of rest demons are looking for, or where they might find it, but whatever it is they must rely upon a human to experience their demon-rest.

In Bishop Bismark's booklet on Prayer, he mentions these hot spots for demonic activity:

- Ganges River, India
- Nile, Egypt
- Tigris, Euphrates Middle East
- Mississippi River, New Orleans
- Thames River, London
- Hudson River, New York
- Bermuda Triangle
- Amazon River

I could add some water hot spots I've observed on my own in my world travels where the occult of pagan worship is strong. In areas such as Hawaii, the Caribbean, and in Seaside resorts around the world you see carnality, flesh, alcohol abuse, drug consumption, and gambling in overdrive.

Getting back to our narrative, let's look at this scripture:

"When an unclean spirit goes out of a man, he goes through dry places, seeking rest, and finds none. Then he says, 'I will return to my house from which I came.' And when he comes, he finds it empty, swept, and put in order. Then he goes and takes with him seven other spirits more wicked than himself, and they enter and dwell there; and the last state of that man is worse than the first. So shall it also be with this wicked generation." (Matthew 25:43-45)

This wandering, restless, vagabond demon that's desperate for a human house can't find a possible candidate in the dry places, so he returns to his former address hoping it isn't filled with the spirit of Christ.

If the earthly house is still vacant, even though swept and put back in order, he decides to get help from seven other spirits more wicked than himself, to hedge his bets. He won't leave as easily as before.

Look at this verse in Contrast:

So He asked his father, "How long has this been happening to him?" And he said, "From childhood. And often he has thrown him both into the fire and into the water to destroy him. But if You can do anything, have compassion on us and help us." Jesus said to him, "If you can believe, all things are possible to him who believes." Immediately the father of the child cried out and said with tears, "Lord, I believe; help my unbelief!" (Mark 9:21-24)

When Jesus saw that the people came running together, He rebuked the unclean spirit, saying to it: "Deaf and dumb spirit, I command you, come out of him and enter him no more!" (Mark 9:25)

Notice, when Jesus casts out a spirit, or even a legion of them, he makes sure they never re-enter the house. We must use our authority in Christ to do likewise.

As we read further in Mark we should take note of a few more important things:

Then the spirit cried out, convulsed him greatly, and came out of him. And he became as one dead, so that many said, "He is dead." But Jesus took him by the hand and lifted him up, and he arose. And when He had come into the house, His disciples asked Him privately, "Why could we not cast it out?" So He said to them, "This kind can come out by nothing but prayer and fasting." (Mark 9:26-29)

There are different kinds of spirits in satan's kingdom. Here's an example of a tormenting demon that was particularly menacing:

And wherever it seizes him, it throws him down; he foams at the mouth, gnashes his teeth, and becomes rigid. So I spoke to Your disciples, that they should cast it out, but they could not. (Mark 9:18)

As I mentioned earlier, in 1982 in Guntar, India during a mass crusade, I had a similar situation. A young girl, maybe eighteen, did exactly the same thing as we see above in Mark.

The demon did come out and a made a literal tearing sound as if paper was being torn. I've never heard such a thing in any of my deliverance opportunities.

I have found some spirits act cowardly and leave instantly. Once, I just stared at a possessed individual without saying a word, and the demon left quietly. Others mock, talk back, taunt, and act confident as if they have the final say. However, they don't, and they never will, but they must be convinced of our resolve, confidence, and God-given authority. They need to know that we're confident that we will always win.

" We shall defend our island, whatever the cost may be, we shall fight on the beaches, we shall fight on the landing grounds, we shall fight in the fields and in the streets, we shall fight in the hills; we shall never surrender."

— *Winston Churchill*

CHAPTER 43

Welcome to the War, Pastor Dick

Then it came to pass, when Pharaoh had let the people go, that God did not lead them by way of the land of the Philistines, although that was near; for God said, "Lest perhaps the people change their minds when they see war, and return to Egypt." So God led the people around by way of the wilderness of the Red Sea. And the children of Israel went up in orderly ranks out of the land of Egypt. (Exodus 13:17-18)

The Philistines were a powerful and warlike race of people who were the masters of the five important cities of Gaza, Ascalon, Ashdad, Gath, and Ekron. These are cities that we frequently read about in the Old Testament. Even though the Israelites may have outnumbered the Philistines, they were unaccustomed to war. What they needed was time, hardship, training. They would get it gradually in the wilderness. Their trek from Tanis to Canaan should have taken six or seven days — maybe a week. Instead, they spent the next forty years getting ready to conquer and occupy the Promise Land.

How long did it take God to prepare planet earth for man? God is never in a hurry even though at times we are. The other day I was growing impatient because the WiFi hook up was taking too many seconds to allow me to load a page.

Have you ever tried to preach patience to children? In this day and age, where delayed gratification is a lost conversation, we no longer celebrate the virtue of patience, even though we love to read about it in the book of James:

> *My brethren, count it all joy when you fall into various trials, knowing that the testing of your faith produces patience. But let patience have its perfect work, that you may be perfect and complete, lacking nothing. (James 1:2-4)*

Reading it is one thing but living it, well, that's another. How do I know? Trust me, after living over seventy years, and pastoring one church for over half that time on earth, I have my stories of frustration at how long one must wait for patience to have it's perfect work.

As a new, born again believer, hair still wet from water baptism, God knows one isn't ready for too much confrontation in the arena of cosmic, spiritual warfare. Exuberance and zeal are no match for the aged and determined powers of darkness who have many scalps hanging from their belts.

The first few years of Jubilee Christian Center were virtually problem-free. Even the San Jose Mercury News did a four-page spread on me, calling me the "Man with the Midas touch." We had the fastest growing church in the history of the Bay Area back in the early 80s. Perhaps God had a hedge of protection around me and told the angels to keep me safe for a learning season. Whatever it was, we were rolling and I thought it would last and be all good. Our first ten years were amazing and relatively stress-free until Halloween night in 1990.

THE WITCH WHO SWITCHED

Back in 1990, Larry Lea, a preacher from Dallas who, at the time was a popular TV personality. Larry taught mostly on prayer and asked us to help him conduct a prayer rally in San Francisco on Halloween night in 1990.

The San Francisco news picked up the story and began broadcasting it on T.V. and in print. They said the upcoming event would draw 10,000 evangelicals to the city on Halloween night.

A celebrity warlock, Eric Pryor, read about our plans and went berserk! "Hell no they're not!" He later told me. He began calling all the pagans together and leaders of the gay community to protest our gathering. He thought it would be a gay-bashing-pagan-hating meeting. Nothing, of course, could be further from the truth, but perception is perception until truth shines the light into darkness.

The media circled around this thing, the rally, and it all got way out of hand. CNN picked up on it. So did the BBC, Europe, Asia, just about every worldwide news source began calling it the "San Francisco Holy War." I remember being interviewed by the Wall Street Journal, News Week, USA Today, NBC, and other outlets I can no longer recall.

We didn't know it at the time, but the downtown venue that was chosen, The Civic Auditorium, was one block from the yearly, Exotica Erotica Ball that was held every Halloween with over 300,000 revelers.

Halloween morning I was invited to be on a CBS morning talk show, "People are Talking," pitted against Eric Pryor, the Wiccan Witch, and Bernie Ward, the "Lion for the Left." Bernie was a KGO radio host who hated me and would let his Bay Area audience know that. It was another circus, to say the least.

I felt like Daniel in the lion's den. I could tell right off the bat, the hosts of the talk show were jaded, being left wing people who disagreed with just about everything I believed.

I tried to say, "We're only here to pray and bless this beautiful city. That's it!" They didn't believe me, of course.

After the live show, I approached Eric. He was dressed in all black and his hair was died white. He was a slip of a man, thin, frail, and very unhealthy looking.

I could see He was scared of me as I towered over him. With a smile, I added, "Eric, can I buy you lunch?" He was floored, I think he thought, I was going to curse him, cuss him out, or hit him.

He nervously said, "Can I bring my girlfriend?"

"Sure, you can bring whoever. Meet me at the Hilton at 1:00 pm," I said.

For about three hours Carla and I shared our testimony, our

heart, and our love for all and for the City of San Francisco. He listened and asked questions.

Finally, I broke out laughing, "Eric, I think I like you." He laughed too. "Hey, come with Carla and me tonight to hear Pastor Larry Lea."

"OK," he agreed.

This is where it get's really interesting. As the evening approached, Carla and I picked up Eric and Sandra and drove to the event. There were already over 3,000 very angry, very drunk Wiccans, Gays, and left wing Anti-Christ groups gathered and ready to rumble. The only thing stopping chaos from breaking out were the Police, Sheriffs, and SWAT teams. Over three-hundred, uniformed officers did their best to control the mob. Still, fights broke out, bottles were thrown, and clothes were torn. In the middle of that angry crowd, we drove up with Eric Pryor (still wearing all black) and Sandra.

When we stepped out of the car and the people that Eric had been rallying all week saw me, they booed like Giants fans do the Dodgers. When Eric got out of the back seat, there was dead silence. Three-thousand shocked faces were dumbfounded. You could tell they were thinking, "what is our leader doing with Bernal?" Eric sheepishly waved at his crowd. At the same time, my church people were staring at me "with a what are you doing with Eric Pryor?" look. It was like a movie scene — surreal to say the least.

Over 7,000 believers packed the auditorium. It was wonderful. We prayed like we were on fire, and Eric felt the power and the love. A week later, he gave his heart to Christ at Jubilee Christian Center, and he remained a Christian until his untimely death in Carson City, Nevada a few years ago.

We stayed in close contact with Eric right until his death. He was truly, "The witch who switched." Of course, the press didn't buy it. Even Diana Sawyer and ABC's *Prime Time Live* thought it was a hoax or a publicity stunt to promote the Christian cause. She slandered me on her show — I now call it *slime-time* — to 11 million people. What amazed me was some church people thought she was right.

Nearly twenty-five years later, people around the world still ask me about that amazing Halloween night in San Francisco, and they ask me if Eric truly got saved.

The principality over the San Francisco area didn't like us bringing in prayer warriors and rescuing Eric Pryor. It was only one night, but clear battle lines were drawn, and they remain ever so clear to this day.

When I visit the City by the Bay, I don't think of Sodom and Gomorrah, I think of Ephesus, a city on a bay much like San Francisco. God's judgment didn't destroy Ephesus. Paul and a handful of believers turned it right side up!

Cities can be won for Christ!

CHAPTER 44

Counting the Cost

Now great multitudes went with Him. And He turned and said to them, "If anyone comes to Me and does not hate his father and mother, wife and children, brothers and sisters, yes, and his own life also, he cannot be My disciple. And whoever does not bear his cross and come after Me cannot be My disciple. For which of you, intending to build a tower, does not sit down first and count the cost, whether he has enough to finish it lest, after he has laid the foundation, and is not able to finish, all who see it begin to mock him, saying, 'This man began to build and was not able to finish'? Or what king, going to make war against another king, does not sit down first and consider whether he is able with ten thousand to meet him who comes against him with twenty thousand? Or else, while the other is still a great way off, he sends a delegation and asks conditions of peace. So likewise, whoever of you does not forsake all that he has cannot be My disciple." (Luke 14:25-33)

There are things our Lord said that raise eyebrows! Like here in our text. Is He commanding us to hate those who are the closest to our heart? No, of course He isn't. However, I think it's obvious that if anyone, father, mother, wife, husband, or friends try to talk us out of following Him and becoming His disciple we are not going to last.

The English word hate here means *love less*. Always compare scripture with scripture. The bible tells us to honor our parents, love our wives as Christ loves the church, respect, and cherish our children. As much as I care for those that are closest to me, none of them will ever talk me out of following my Lord until the day I die.

When I first was called, many tried to talk sense into me. I had a new life, a wife, a child, and a good paying union job as an ironworker. We owned a nice little house and we had great friends. When I told my family I was leaving it all behind, packing up and heading to bible school in Tulsa, Oklahoma they thought I had lost my mind. In the natural it did look crazy, I agree, but when you give it all to Jesus, He will reward you.

While in Tulsa, I worked the graveyard shift at a convenience store, called Get-N-Go where I was robbed by thugs, threatened by drunks, hit on by a teenage prostitute and a gay man, and cursed out by angry customers. I had to learn how to drive on freezing black ice, I ran out of gas... and that is the short list!

I only made $3.79 an hour and I worked sixty hours a week. Carla was pregnant with Jesse, and we were both attending Rhema Bible Training Center, four hours a day, five days a week. I have to admit, at times I thought I was crazy, but I was determined to serve God however He saw fit to use me.

That was a time of constant warfare, but it toughened me up and got me ready for what lay ahead.

Going back to our narrative, Jesus used two striking examples of discipleship: (1) building a tower, and (2) planning an attack.

The tower speaks of defense, protection, and observation. War speaks of offense, provision, and occupation. A true disciple of Christ understands the importance of both.

Our Lord's stern warning is this: Don't start until you have really thought it through, then, if you choose to follow and to be a disciple, there's no turning back!

Jesus added and I paraphrase, "People are watching." Jesus is not looking for crowds, members, or fans. He's looking for builders, warriors, and disciples who will persevere through hell, high water, and whatever else is thrown at them.

Let's look at the sixth chapter of John:

After these things Jesus went over the Sea of Galilee, which is the Sea of Tiberias. Then a great multitude followed Him, because they saw His signs which He performed on those who were diseased. And Jesus went up on the mountain, and there He sat with His disciples. Now the Passover, a feast of the Jews, was near. Then Jesus lifted up His eyes, and seeing a great multitude coming toward Him, He said to Philip, "Where shall we buy bread, that these may eat?" But this He said to test him, for He Himself knew what He would do. (John 6:1-6)

Philip answered Him, "Two hundred denarii worth of bread is not sufficient for them, that every one of them may have a little." One of His disciples, Andrew, Simon Peter's brother, said to Him, "There is a lad here who has five barley loaves and two small fish, but what are they among so many?" Then Jesus said, "Make the people sit down." Now there was much grass in the place. So the men sat down, in number about five thousand. And Jesus took the loaves, and when He had given thanks He distributed them to the disciples, and the disciples to those sitting down; and likewise of the fish, as much as they wanted. So when they were filled, He said to His disciples, "Gather up the fragments that remain, so that nothing is lost." Therefore they gathered them up, and filled twelve baskets with the fragments of the five barley loaves which were left over by those who had eaten. Then those men, when they had seen the sign that Jesus did, said, "This is truly the Prophet who is to come into the world." (John 6:7-14)

This is one of the great miracles of our Lord's ministry. What movie about Jesus doesn't have this amazing scene in it?

What was going through the minds of the people? Is this the new Moses who fed our forefathers and families for forty years. The free lunch is back, Hallelujah!

Look at verse fifteen:

Therefore when Jesus perceived that they were about to come and take Him by force to make Him king, He departed again to the mountain by Himself alone. (John 6:15)

As the story goes, the crowd kept following or looking for Him. But he ditched them on purpose. Let's keep reading:

And when they found Him on the other side of the sea, they said to Him, "Rabbi, when did You come here?" Jesus answered them and said, "Most assuredly, I say to you, you seek Me, not because you saw the signs, but because you ate of the loaves and were filled. Do not labor for the food which perishes, but for the food which endures to everlasting life, which the Son of Man will give you, because God the Father has set His seal on Him." Then they said to Him, "What shall we do, that we may work the works of God?" Jesus answered and said to them, "This is the work of God, that you believe in Him whom He sent." Therefore they said to Him, "What sign will You perform then, that we may see it and believe You? What work will You do? Our fathers ate the manna in the desert; as it is written, 'He gave them bread from heaven to eat.'" (John 6:25-31)

You would think Jesus, the prophet and preacher, would love having a crowd follow Him. Today, with mega-churches and celebrity ministers, we are amazed at how big some ministries are. But here, Jesus' ministry isn't that big.

Let's continue reading:

Then Jesus said to them, "Most assuredly, I say to you, Moses did not give you the bread from heaven, but My Father gives you the true bread from heaven. For the bread of God is He who comes down from heaven and gives life to the world." Then they said to Him, "Lord, give us this bread always." And Jesus said to them, "I am the bread of life. He who comes to Me shall never hunger, and he who believes in Me shall never thirst. But I said to you that you have seen Me and yet do not believe. All that the Father gives Me will come to Me, and the one who comes to Me I will by no means cast out. For I have come down from heaven, not to do My own will, but the will of Him who sent Me. This is the will of the Father who sent Me, that of all He has given Me I should lose nothing, but should raise it up at the last day. And this is the will of Him who sent Me, that everyone who sees the Son and believes in Him may have everlasting life; and I will raise him up at the last day." (John 6:32-40)

Apparently the crowd is focused upon food and miracles, not upon a spiritual lecture.

Now He cuts to the chase:

Then Jesus said to them, "Most assuredly, I say to you, unless you eat the flesh of the Son of Man and drink His blood, you have no life in you. Whoever eats My flesh and drinks My blood has eternal life, and I will raise him up at the last day. For My flesh is food indeed, and My blood is drink indeed. He who eats My flesh and drinks My blood abides in Me, and I in him. As the living Father sent Me, and I live because of the Father, so he who feeds on Me will live because of Me. This is the bread which came down from heaven—not as your fathers ate the manna, and are dead. He who eats this bread will live forever." These things He said in the synagogue as He taught in Capernaum. (John 6:53-59)

I've said some things over the years that offended a few people, and they left our church, but I never had the whole congregation get up and walk out! He's left with the original twelve who are not sure they want to stay.

In our modern world, the happy, feel good, positive-can-do messages can fill up a church. In this age, selling Jesus on the easy installment plan resonates with the masses. I'm all for getting seekers into our churches. However, with the dark days that are surely ahead, we need to teach our church members spiritual warfare tactics. Otherwise, they won't last.

Jesus, in Mark chapter 4, lays it out plainly — no deep roots, no lasting fruits:

> *And He said to them, "Do you not understand this parable? How then will you understand all the parables? The sower sows the word. And these are the ones by the wayside where the word is sown. When they hear, Satan comes immediately and takes away the word that was sown in their hearts. These likewise are the ones sown on stony ground who, when they hear the word, immediately receive it with gladness; and they have no root in themselves, and so endure only for a time. Afterward, when tribulation or persecution arises for the word's sake, immediately they stumble. Now these are the ones sown among thorns; they are the ones who hear the word, and the cares of this world, the deceitfulness of riches, and the desires for other things entering in choke the word, and it becomes unfruitful. But these are the ones sown on good ground, those who hear the word, accept it, and bear fruit: some thirtyfold, some sixty, and some a hundred." (Mark 4:13-20)*

" You will find peace
not by trying to
escape your problems,
but by confronting
them courageously.
You will find peace
not in denial, but
in victory."
— *J. Donald Walters*

CHAPTER 45

Place of the Skull

In the iconic story of David and Goliath, we saw, what appeared on the surface a mad enterprise. Here, a youth perhaps fifteen, who's given to music, poetry, and gentle pursuits, should entertain the foolish notion he was suited for such an impossible task. Even his older brother, the firstborn of Jesse, scolds him and tries to send him home:

> *Then David spoke to the men who stood by him, saying, "What shall be done for the man who kills this Philistine and takes away the reproach from Israel? For who is this uncircumcised Philistine, that he should defy the armies of the living God?" And the people answered him in this manner, saying, "So shall it be done for the man who kills him." Now Eliab his oldest brother heard when he spoke to the men; and Eliab's anger was aroused against David, and he said, "Why did you come down here? And with whom have you left those few sheep in the wilderness? I know your pride and the insolence of your heart, for you have come down to see the battle." And David said, "What have*

I done now? Is there not a cause?" Then he turned from him toward another and said the same thing; and these people answered him as the first ones did. (1 Samuel 17:26-29)

"Is there not a cause." What an answer! Likewise, King Saul tries to discourage David from this insanity:

Now when the words which David spoke were heard, they reported them to Saul; and he sent for him. Then David said to Saul, "Let no man's heart fail because of him; your servant will go and fight with this Philistine." And Saul said to David, "You are not able to go against this Philistine to fight with him; for you are a youth, and he a man of war from his youth. (1 Samuel 17:31-33)

But, once again, David's resolve comes to the fore:

But David said to Saul, "Your servant used to keep his father's sheep, and when a lion or a bear came and took a lamb out of the flock, I went out after it and struck it, and delivered the lamb from its mouth; and when it arose against me, I caught it by its beard, and struck and killed it. Your servant has killed both lion and bear; and this uncircumcised Philistine will be like one of them, seeing he has defied the armies of the living God." Moreover David said, "The Lord, who delivered me from the paw of the lion and from the paw of the bear, He will deliver me from the hand of this Philistine." And Saul said to David, "Go, and the Lord be with you!" (1 Samuel 17:34-37)

David was skilled with the harp as well as with his slingshot. He was tender with his shepherd's staff, but it also would come in handy as a club against predators. Yet, still, a lion and a bear is one thing, but a giant warrior is quite another! Was Goliath some of the last of the Nephthalim recorded in Genesis 6, who later were called the Anakims:

Nevertheless the people who dwell in the land are strong; the cities are fortified and very large; moreover we saw the descendants of Anak there. The Amalekites dwell in the land of the South; the Hittites, the Jebusites, and the Amorites dwell in the mountains; and the Canaanites dwell by the sea and along the banks of the Jordan." Then Caleb quieted the people before Moses, and said, "Let us go up at once and take possession, for we are well able to overcome it." But the men who had gone up with him said, "We are not able to go up against the people, for they are stronger than we." And they gave the children of Israel a bad report of the land which they had spied out, saying, "The land through which we have gone as spies is a land that devours its inhabitants, and all the people whom we saw in it are men of great stature. There we saw the giants (the descendants of Anak came from the giants); and we were like grasshoppers in our own sight, and so we were in their sight." (Numbers 33:28-33)

There was a time when freakish giants walked the earth bringing fear and dread to any who saw them as adversaries.

David was oblivious to Goliath's stature, experience, or even his armor and weapons. David was well aware of God's prophecy to Abram in Genesis 12:1-3:

> *Now the Lord had said to Abram:*
> *"Get out of your country, from your family and from your father's house, to a land that I will show you. I will make you a great nation; I will bless you and make your name great; and you shall be a blessing. I will bless those who bless you, and I will curse him who curses you; and in you all the families of the earth shall be blessed."*

Goliath had been cursing the children of Israel for forty days and nights. David had more faith in the power of God than fear at the sight of Goliath, knowing covenant and its mark, he says:

> *Then David spoke to the men who stood by him, saying, "What shall be done for the man who kills this Philistine and takes away the reproach from Israel? For who is this uncircumcised Philistine, that he should defy the armies of the living God? (1 Samuel 17:26)*

David used a rock and a slingshot to rid Israel of its foe:

> *Therefore David ran and stood over the Philistine, took his sword and drew it out of its sheath and killed him, and cut off his head with it. And when the Philistines saw that their champion was dead, they fled. Now the men of Israel and Judah arose and shouted, and pursued the Philistines as far as the entrance of the valley and to*

the gates of Ekron. And the wounded of the Philistines fell along the road to Shaaraim, even as far as Gath and Ekron. Then the children of Israel returned from chasing the Philistines, and they plundered their tents. And David took the head of the Philistine and brought it to Jerusalem, but he put his armor in his tent. (1 Samuel 17:51-54)

We, today, stand on the rock of our salvation and use the Word of God in our mouth like a sword of the Spirit

What did David eventually do with the head of Goliath? Many have suggested that he buried it outside of Jerusalem in a place later called, "The Place of the Skull or Golgatha." Doesn't Golgatha sound like Goliath of Gath? If so, how powerful is that image of our Lord crucified on top of Golgatha (Calvary) and the cross crushing the head of satan, which was prophesied by God way back in Genesis 3:14-15. To *bruise your head* literally means to *crush your headship and power.*

One last thought before we move on to our summary: this battle between the Philistines and Israel took place in the Valley of Elah:

And Saul and the men of Israel were gathered together, and they encamped in the Valley of Elah, and drew up in battle array against the Philistines. The Philistines stood on a mountain on one side, and Israel stood on a mountain on the other side, with a valley between them. (1 Samuel 17:2-3)

Elah has several meanings. One meaning is *strong tree*. Think about it! David defeated Goliath in the Valley of Elah… Jesus, hung on a tree and forever reversed satan's curse:

For as many as are of the works of the law are under the curse; for it is written, "Cursed is everyone who does not continue in all things which are written in the book of the law, to do them." But that no one is justified by the law in the sight of God is evident, for "the just shall live by faith." Yet the law is not of faith, but "the man who does them shall live by them." Christ has redeemed us from the curse of the law, having become a curse for us (for it is written, "Cursed is everyone who hangs on a tree", that the blessing of Abraham might come upon the Gentiles in Christ Jesus, that we might receive the promise of the Spirit through faith. (Galatians 3:10-14)

CHAPTER 46

Summary

And Moses said to the people, "Do not be afraid. Stand still, and see the salvation of the Lord, which He will accomplish for you today. For the Egyptians whom you see today, you shall see again no more forever. The Lord will fight for you, and you shall hold your peace." And the Lord said to Moses, "Why do you cry to Me? Tell the children of Israel to go forward. (Exodus 14:13-15)

And he said, "Listen, all you of Judah and you inhabitants of Jerusalem, and you, King Jehoshaphat! Thus, says the Lord to you: 'Do not be afraid nor dismayed because of this great multitude, for the battle is not yours, but God's. Tomorrow go down against them. They will surely come up by the Ascent of Ziz, and you will find them at the end of the brook before the Wilderness of Jeruel. You will not need to fight in this battle. Position yourselves, stand still and see the salvation of the Lord, who is with you, O Judah and Jerusalem!' Do not fear or be dismayed; tomorrow go out against them, for the Lord is with you." (2 Chronicles 20:15-17)

These passages are reminders of the big picture. The battle, this daily, ongoing struggle of good vs. the forces of satan and his minions is called "The Lord's Battle!" If we are serious believers doing our best to walk by faith and love, and live by God's word, hell will rise up against us.

Satan is the original night stalker. He will use every means at his disposal to bring darkness into our lives, our marriages, our families, our workplace, and, of course, in our churches if he can find a crack in our armor, or a door left unlocked.

I've been attacked in all those areas, as have so many of you who are reading this book. Oh, I almost left out some challenges I've had with my personal finances and my health. Yet at seventy-three years of age, nearly forty years of serving God and God's people, I'm still standing strong!

> **In fear, I stand.**
> **In lack, I stand.**
> **In times of trouble, I stand.**
> **People forsaking me, I stand.**
> **Having done all to stand, I must keep standing!**

Standing still and trusting God has not been easy at times. There have been more than a few times I "jumped the gun," as we used to say and tried to hurry the process along. God was not moving fast enough, in my opinion, and, boy, did I suffer for being impatient.

Hebrews tells us, faith works best while we are at rest, when true peace and joy can quiet the mind and soul. However, standing still does not mean we have no role in the battle.

In Exodus and 2 Chronicles, God said, "Stand still and see the salvation of the Lord." And then added, "Move forward."

Even young David ran directly at his giant problem, knowing the battle was really the Lord's. However, his obedience and raw faith prevailed.

In Isaiah, there's a passage that God wanted, and still to this day, wants Satan to take personally:

"But I know your dwelling place, your going out and your coming in, and your rage against Me. Because your rage against Me and your tumult have come up to My ears, therefore I will put My hook in your nose and My bridle in your lips, and I will turn you back by the way which you came." By the way that he came, by the same shall he return; and he shall not come into this city,' says the Lord. 'For I will defend this city, to save it, for My own sake and for My servant David's sake.'" *(Isaiah 37:28-29 and 34-35)*

My final thought can be summed up in this beautiful Psalm:

God is our refuge and strength,
A very present help in trouble.
Therefore we will not fear,
Even though the earth be removed,
And though the mountains be carried
into the midst of the sea;
Though its waters roar and be troubled,
Though the mountains shake with its swelling. Selah
There is a river whose streams shall

make glad the city of God,
The holy place of the tabernacle of the Most High.
God is in the midst of her, she shall not be moved;
God shall help her, just at the break of dawn.
The nations raged, the kingdoms were moved;
He uttered His voice, the earth melted.
The Lord of hosts is with us;
The God of Jacob is our refuge. Selah
Come, behold the works of the Lord,
Who has made desolations in the earth.
He makes wars cease to the end of the earth;
He breaks the bow and cuts the spear in two;
He burns the chariot in the fire.
Be still, and know that I am God;
I will be exalted among the nations,
I will be exalted in the earth!
The Lord of hosts is with us;
The God of Jacob is our refuge. Selah
(Psalm 46:1-11)

This book contains strategies I have learned through experience, and principles I have learned from the word of God, as well as wisdom I have gleaned from God. However, when you find yourself in a uniquely challenging situation, call upon your ever-present helper, teacher, and guide, the Holy Spirit of Truth.

I would love to hear from you. Please share your victory testimonies with me.

" Battle is the most magnificent competition in which a human being can indulge. It brings out all that is best; it removes all that is base. All men are afraid in battle. The coward is the one who lets his fear overcome his sense of duty. Duty is the essence of manhood."
— *George S. Patton*